THE PEDRO GORINO

THE PEDRO GORINO

The Adventures of a Negro Sea-Captain in Africa and on the Seven Seas in his attempts to Found an Ethiopian Empire

An Autobiographical Narrative

By

CAPTAIN HARRY DEAN

WRITTEN WITH THE ASSISTANCE OF
STERLING NORTH

INTRODUCTION BY
STERLING LECATER BLAND, JR.

WESTHOLME
Yardley

Introduction © 2011 Westholme Publishing
Originally published by Houghton Mifflin Company, 1929
First Westholme paperback 2011

Westholme Publishing, LLC
904 Edgewood Road
Yardley, Pennsylvania 19067
Visit our Web site at www.westholmepublishing.com
First Printing May 2011
10 9 8 7 6 5 4 3 2 1
ISBN: 978-1-59416-135-3
Also available as an eBook.

Printed in the United States of America.

TO

KING SEGOW FAKU
QUEEN BARING
THE ILLUSTRIOUS
MISS MONYE
AND MY OTHER FRIENDS
IN AFRICA

INTRODUCTION

BLACK EMPIRE: PAN-AFRICANISM, CAPTAIN HARRY DEAN, AND THE *Pedro Gorino*

> One three centuries removed
> From scenes his fathers loved
> Spicy grove and cinnamon tree,
> What is Africa to me?
> —Countee Cullen, "Heritage"

> Africa is at once the most romantic and the
> most tragic of continents.
> —W.E.B. Du Bois, *The Negro*

Captain Harry Foster Dean's autobiographical narrative is a unique and powerful account of international travel and adventure. It provides a compelling and important record of his attempts to counteract the effects of European colonialism by purchasing and governing land in Africa with the intention of establishing a sovereign black homeland. More broadly, it was Harry Dean's vision to provide the economic and social basis upon which blacks—both in Africa and throughout the diaspora—could ultimately expel European colonial influence entirely from the African continent and make it possible for blacks from around the world to return to what he saw as their spiritual and cultural homeland.

Harry Dean was certainly not the first to consider the possibility of black emigration to Africa or the creation of an independent nation governed by blacks. The abolitionist Alexander Crummell, for example, was a staunch advocate of pan-African thought during the nineteenth century. Crummell regularly preached that black Christians living in the Caribbean and in the United States had a particular responsibility to return to Africa to convert native Africans to Christianity. His larger plan, which never fully came to fruition, was to use the tools of religious conversion and education (starting in Liberia) as the basis for establishing a black led republican government. At the end of the nineteenth century, the writer Sutton Elbert Griggs also envisioned the possibility of black political control in his novel *Imperium in Imperio* ("Empire within an Empire"), which imagined a utopian world in which blacks constructed a separate black-controlled government within the borders of the United States. Seen in this context, Harry Dean's work incorporates these perspectives and looks toward the influences of twentieth-century black nationalists and pan-Africanists like Marcus Garvey and W.E.B Du Bois. Because of this, Harry Dean's autobiography occupies what is for some a peculiar position in the progression of nationalist thought. It links nineteenth century back-to-Africa movements with the pan-Africanist movements that emerged in the early portion of the twentieth century.

When considered from a broader perspective, Harry Dean's autobiography actually participates in a much larger conversation among African Americans about the relationship of blacks living throughout the diaspora to Africa itself. During the years when Harry Dean was sailing the globe, the social and political advances initiated during Reconstruction were in the process of being reversed or dismantled altogether. In a period characterized by pervasive anti-black rhetoric and public policy throughout the United States, the attractions of Africa were obvious. Africa provided a compellingly influential geographic and sociopolitical landscape upon which African Americans could map a cultural past characterized by African achievement and a cultural future that assured equally auspicious accomplishment. In short, Africa offered a forceful counter-narrative to a present that was compromised by pervasive racism, educational limitation, economic hardship, and political disenfranchisement. Africa provided an important space that African Americans could use as a focal point for relieving the tensions and contradictions that were so entwined with black cultural aspiration in the United States.

Much of what contemporary readers know about Harry Dean comes from his own autobiography. The details of the autobiography's composition raise a number of important questions. In the introduction to the book, Sterling North writes about being a twenty-year-old student at the University of Chicago when a faculty member introduced him to Harry Dean in March of 1928. North was asked to help Dean compose his autobiography, which he did based entirely on Dean's recollections. At the time of the autobiography's composition, Dean was a sixty-three-year-old man who, by his own estimate, had gained and lost a fortune three times in his

life. He came to Sterling North with lots of stories but little to offer in the way of evidence or substantive factual
support.

Harry Dean says he was born in Philadelphia in 1864
and claims a familial connection to Paul Cuffe, who was
the grandfather of Dean's mother. Cuffe was a free black
man who was born on January 17, 1759 in Chuttyhunk,
Massachusetts. He learned how to sail, owned ships, and
became very prosperous by trading goods around the
world. He became a strong proponent of the American
Colonization Society. By 1816, Cuffe had conceptualized
an emigration plan that saw the idea of black emigration
to Sierra Leone and the newly-formed Republic of Haiti,
which had recently won its freedom from France, as the
most viable way to empower American blacks. Like Paul
Cuffe, Harry Dean claims to have learned how to sail at
a young age and says that he quickly recognized the
important relationship between sailing and black political sovereignty and economic self-determination. As an
indication of his dedication to black advancement,
Harry Dean includes the story of his trip to London in
1900 where he attended the Pan-African congress and
met W.E.B. Du Bois.

After purchasing the *Pedro Gorino*, Harry Dean made
his living as a trader and remained committed to finding
a territory in Africa where a sovereign black nation
could be established. Astonishingly enough, Dean
asserts that he was offered the area of Mozambique but
was unable to secure funding from the black Americans
whom he approached for support. Dean says that he was
later able to secure a commitment from local leaders to

purchase a parcel of land in what was then known as Basutoland. In the years following the end of the Boer Wars, Dean began to assemble the teachers, craftsmen, planters, and others whose work he felt would be necessary for the establishment of a successful new African nation. His plans were derailed when he says that he was tricked into buying goods on credit for his new nation. He presented the *Pedro Gorino* as collateral. He lost his life savings when his warehouse burned and his fortune in goods was destroyed. Dean found himself in debt that he could not repay. He was given the choice of serving time in prison for the debt or signing over his ship and his parcel of land and leaving South Africa. Dean chose to sign over his ship, relinquish his parcel of land, and leave. His return to the United States in 1914 was marked by disappointment. Dean briefly settled in Chicago before relocating to California. In California, he tried unsuccessfully to convince American businessmen to open trade relationships with West Africa and he tried to purchase another ship. He was hindered by discrimination and lack of capital. He returned to Chicago in the years preceding the Depression and began the process of dictating his autobiography to Sterling North. Harry Dean died in 1935.

Harry Dean's is clearly a fascinating story of seafaring adventure combined with a pan-Africanist worldview. One of the questions regularly directed at the narrative (and more broadly toward African American narrative writing in general) is the question of truth and accuracy. Dean's narrative primarily looks back toward the first forty years of his life. Since the narrative was dictated more than twenty years after the conclusion of the events contained in the narrative, it is entirely possible that Dean embellished or simply forgot some of the details of his experiences. According to George Shepperson, who wrote an introduction to a British edition of Harry Dean's narrative that was published in England in 1989 under the title *Umbala*, Dean was a bit guarded about sharing his diaries. But Shepperson also stresses that while Dean may have romanticized his experiences a bit, he felt no sense that Dean "consciously lied or intended to deceive." In his 1973 master's thesis on the subject, John S. Berger similarly concludes that Dean's autobiographical narrative did not seem to be a conscious attempt to mislead or fabricate.

Perhaps what unnecessarily complicates our reading of the narrative is the insistence on whether or not Dean consciously provided false or otherwise embellished information. The life story that Dean presents his reader is a striking example of the kind of double consciousness that W.E.B. Du Bois had notably described at the opening of *The Souls of Black Folk* in 1903. One portion of that consciousness reflects the anxieties of race in America at a time that limited the full participation of African Americans in all aspects of social, political, and economic life in the United States. The decades at the end of the nineteenth century are characterized by the rise of the Ku Klux Klan, increasing vigilante violence against blacks, judicial rulings that institutionalized "separate but equal" daily experiences for blacks and whites, and the institutionalization of numerous economic and social barriers. To some extent, this strand of racial identity functions around the ways white people view and respond to African Americans. But the other strand of Du Bois's conception of double consciousness focuses on the other side of the veil, where the anxieties of racial consciousness centered on the ways blacks conceptualized themselves in the larger context of the American mainstream. In other words, the struggle that African Americans faced was to find a way to reconstruct derogatory ideologies of race into a complimentary vision of American identity. This version of black uplift, at least as Du Bois saw it at the turn of the twentieth century, emphasized some melding of the African with the American. Du Bois writes in the opening pages of *The Souls of Black Folk* that "He would not Africanize America, for America has too much to teach the world and Africa. He would not bleach his Negro soul in a flood of white Americanism, for he knows that Negro blood has a message for the world. He simply wishes to make it possible for a man to be both a Negro and an American, without being cursed and spit on by his fellows, without having the doors of Opportunity closed roughly in his face." Du Bois uses this conception of double-consciousness as a kind of shorthand for the relationship of Africa and America that Du Bois sees as being crucial to black uplift. But for those, like Harry Dean, who were most invested in and enthusiastic about the idea of a bright future rooted in a direct connection to Africa, the thought of synthesizing America with Africa was troubling. From this perspective, the emphasis should have been on creating opportunity rather than on seeking assimilation and requesting concession.

W.E.B. Du Bois's thoughts on race certainly developed and changed during his long and illustrious career, but this version of racial uplift functions on the belief that uplift was as much a function of culture as it was a function of race. This interpretation of racial uplift sought to reform the race through the lens of the white gaze and in doing so implicitly echoed mainstream cultural beliefs about the "Negro problem" by assigning responsibility for the racial inferiority of blacks in the United States on blacks themselves. In other words, the status of blacks was not, as the argument had been made earlier in the nineteenth century, biologically determined at all. Instead, the status of blacks was socially determined. So the primary task for improving the status of blacks involved an emphasis on widely-held values like racial unity, economic development, financial independence, patriarchial influence, and the adoption of middle class values. From this perspective, African Americans were no different than other immigrant communities in that assimilation and the combining of the African with the American was a viable strategy for social advancement.

Harry Dean's narrative offered an important pan-African counter narrative to this strategy for addressing the inferior status of blacks in the United States and throughout the diaspora. Harry Dean's autobiography specifically focused on Africa's role as a center of civilization and saw the reestablishment of a vibrant African past as being vital to the creation of a viable pan-African future. In this regard, Dean's autobiographical narrative speaks toward his understanding of Africa as a geopolitical space upon which he could map his beliefs about racial aspiration and cultural advancement.

Although Harry Dean's life story cannot be fully corroborated, his autobiographical narrative stands as an exciting collection of stories from locations around the world. Harry Dean's narrative reflects his lifelong mission to promote trans-Atlantic commerce between Africa and the United States as a way of constructing independence, uplifting the black race, and reestablishing a black controlled homeland in Africa. It is an important and under-studied contribution to the discussion of Africa's relationship to the African American liberation movement.

STERLING LECATER BLAND, JR.

April 2011

PREFACE

THIS is the true story of a 'negro' sea captain's adventures. It is only through lucky coincidence that it has been set down and preserved, for if Captain Harry Dean had not lost his ship he would still be sailing the sea. All his life he has been a 'sea tramp, a fellow that cries at the sight of land.' If now at the age of sixty-three he is also an author extraordinary, it is because the poetry of the wind and the sea fills his veins and he cannot choose but sing.

On Thursday, March 1, 1928, Miss Gladys Finn, Director of Activities at the University of Chicago, called me into her office to meet this charming old man. He had come to Chicago and, unable to find employment of any kind, had thrown himself on the mercy of Professors Ames and Mead, for, as he himself said, 'Plato was right about philosophers being the best rulers and the only really generous class of men.' I had been called in to help Captain Dean with his life's story, and although it was tremendously exciting I thought how incapable I was of such a task. I had published a few poems and stories in various magazines, and I had had three years of college work — there was little else to recommend me. But what a glorious adventure! It was his first book and mine, he a poet of sixty-three, I one of twenty.

On that first afternoon, as we walked about the campus in the cold March sunshine, he talked of Africa, inland mountains where multicolored birds

sang in unbelievable foliage.   He told of days when
there still were pirates on the seas, of battles he had
seen, of storm and shipwreck.   We were no longer on
the cold campus in the pale sunshine; we were aboard
his good ship Pedro Gorino ploughing southward
under full sail for Cape Town with the sea birds flock-
ing along behind.   We dropped anchor at the mouths
of jungle rivers and watched the black, sinewy bodies
of young 'negroes' coming aboard hand over hand.   I
had lost all sense of time and space.   We were crossing
Africa by moonlight to the sound of drums, we were
being pursued down a vine-entangled path.

'I look like a poor old man,' he said, 'but I am a
prince in my own right back in Africa.   I know things
that would make the King of England tremble on his
throne.   I know facts that would make the imperialists
of every nation blush with shame.   And yet I can't
get money enough to keep soul and body together.
Listen,' he said; 'I know the history of Africa sixteen
thousand years.   Why, I am blood brother to more
than one king.   There is not a drop of slave blood in
my body.'   He had trailed off into another subject, and
it was growing dark.

Perhaps the best description I can give of this man
is one in an article by Professor A. E. Anderson, of the
University of California, which appeared in the *Post
Inquirer* of Oakland, California, for July 26, 1923:

One of the most interesting personalities I have met in a
long time is a 'negro' sea captain named Harry Dean. . . .
His face is a striking brown and straight-chiseled; the mouth
firm and remarkably well formed, with a strange upward
lift at the corners of the lips; the eyes deep and brooding; and

deeply scarred across the forehead and cut downward across the cheeks and scattered in a fine tracery over the entire face are wrinkles made by time, and wrinkles made by thought, and wrinkles seamed into the flesh by suffering. The hair is quite white, but a little black mustache with a Parisian lift gives an odd touch of youthfulness to the features. If I were a sculptor, I should like to model that face.

Captain Dean talks easily and well, without the faintest suggestion of a dialect. His choice of words is picturesque and expressive, his English remarkably correct. I sat listening to him for two hours, watching the play of his eager features and my interest did not flag. It was a fascinating tale he told me of adventures all over the world, in the jungles, before the mast, and in most of the capitals of Europe....

He has changed somewhat since that description was written. He has grown older, the mustache is gone; but the fountain of bright words flows in an uninterrupted stream.

We met again on a Saturday, and he told me briefly his whole story, such a story as one might never hear again. There was something infinitely glamorous about the old captain. He was sitting so that the afternoon light fell on his strong features and white hair, making his face, which is the color of Guinea gold, shine with pale iridescence. He told me of his ancestors who were seamen, Said Kafu who had saved the life of McKinnon Paige, a pirate captain, thereby winning that gentleman's lifelong devotion. Of Paul Cuffee and his great brig the Traveler. Of his own early trip to sea, his years of hardship the world over, and, finally, of his great adventure, his attempt to found an Ethiopian Empire. There was a faint note of bitterness when he spoke of his life spent in the thankless toil of helping his race. Yet he was still idealistic and many of his remarks proved that he still hoped to realize his great ambition.

Here was fate in its most ironical mood. That this man, by lineage and by nature an aristocrat, should be unable to secure so much as a meal or a place to sleep may seem hard to believe, but a little more than four months ago he was in that situation. He had known Cecil Rhodes, Conrad, Sir Alfred Milner, and scores of men as important; he had made and lost three great fortunes; yet when I met him he was walking the street penniless. It is little wonder that I was attracted at once. Not only his romantic stories, more poetry than prose, but his nature, fine and sensitive as a child's beneath the stern exterior, made me wish to help him and to know him better.

His whole life has been a quest. Like Arthur's knights, he has searched the world over for a grail, and, like those warriors of other years, he has searched in vain. For him the grail has been a vision of ships, a vision of the colored race come into its own. In his own words, 'A nation without ships is like a man stricken and blind. A country must have ships to live. Remember Phœnicia, Venice, and Spain in their power. That is why I have spent my life finding bright boys to learn navigation. But it doesn't pay to learn the secret of power. Life hates me for having reduced all human progression to a single premise.'

In many ways the story of the Pedro Gorino symbolizes his quest. She was a slick two-masted topsail schooner with a freak rigging, and he loved her as much as his life. It seemed to him that the African fleet had its little nucleus and that it was merely a matter of years before his dream would be a reality. But while he captained his boat along the coasts of Africa, there were other forces at work over which he had no control. The Boer War and the subsequent action of the British Government were to play a bigger rôle than he had suspected. The tragedy of the story is not unlike the tragedy of his whole life.

In his fifty years of adventure, Captain Dean has circumnavigated Africa eighteen times, crossed it from east to west three times and from north to south once. He has been shot, cut, thrown overboard, and almost hanged. On several occasions he has been imprisoned and throughout his life he has known great hardship. To bear up under such a strain he has of necessity developed a philosophy. I was puzzled for some weeks to know just what that philosophy was, but as we talked together day after day it became increasingly clear that he is a fatalist. Like other men of the sea and wilderness whose contact with nature has taught them their own impotence, Captain Dean has found himself nothing but a pawn in a game he cannot control.

Above all he is ardently pro-African. He denies very heatedly the existence of cannibal tribes and defies any African explorer to point out a true case of cannibalism. He attributes the widespread belief to three sources: the habit of lying about one's enemies — tribes often speak of their neighbors as cannibals for want of a worse insult; the rite of eating certain portions of slain enemies — this is quite as symbolic as the Lord's Supper with Christians and is believed to promote valor and courage; the existence of crazed individuals even in Africa — since there are no asylums to hold them, these people may commit atrocities of every nature. But he defies any one to find tribes of natives who capture men for food. And with food so plentiful none are driven to this extremity. He also denies the stories of promiscuity among these people, and claims that in the regions where they are not in contact with the Europeans, and where the native code of morals is unimpaired, adultery is often punished with death.

He feels that in civilization man is restricted and suppressed, but in the wildernesses of Africa he at least has a fighting chance to make a living. As he puts it: 'Men in the Western civilization are prisoners and slaves. They waste their lives in a vain effort to retain the right to labor in the factories and the mines, and are forever within the grasp of fellow men. In Africa I can go out any morning when the dew is on the grass and almost without taking aim shoot enough doves for my dinner. The so-called barbarian is free, and

> "Rich as a king when at the close of day
> Home to his cot he takes his happy way,
> And on his table spreads his simple fare
> Drawn from the meadow without cost or care." '

Captain Dean feels that the word 'negro' is of false derivation, undescriptive, and in every way unfit for the position it fills in our language. He claims that there is no 'negro' race, only many African races. He has written over ten thousand words on the subject, and has convinced me that in a degree he is right.

For this reason we have enclosed the word in quotation marks wherever it appears in the story.

While he was still a child, Captain Dean was put under the tutelage of Fannie Jackson, the famous 'negro' woman educator. He learned the science of navigation some years later in England. For fifty years he has been studying intensely in his own way. The sea has taught him much, but he has not entrusted all his development to direct experience. He says that he has read over five thousand books, and he quotes from a score of poets and philosophers. On one occasion when we were starting a new chapter he said, 'We had better read again our "Casanova," "Monte Cristo," and "Benvenuto Cellini" before we tackle this chapter. There is nothing like studying the method of the great ones.' Horace is his favorite poet, and he always carries a book of his poems in his pocket. He tells me that he has had access to manuscripts the Western world has never seen.

'The Pedro Gorino' is an autobiography of Captain Dean's life as closely as he can remember it. If something has been lost in the telling, it is perhaps no little wonder, for we have had absolutely no system in writing the book. Some of it has come directly from his pen, some he has dictated to me, but every word is the true story of his adventures. For fear some one might think an old sea captain incapable of the poetical passages throughout the book, let me quote a few sentences just as he handed them to me in his delightful script:

Far out on the wild Atlantic we had no thought of the Biscayan tides but were surrounded by porpoises even before we came to cloudless Madeira and the pearl Teneriffe, set as they were in a sea of glass. . . .

Was it any wonder that I wished to save my friend? To have his free spirit and adventurous nature cooped within prison walls was like clipping the wings of a brilliant cock, or harnessing a stallion to the plough. . . .

We passed outside the island only sighting her hills. The menacing sky kept us on the alert, but the splendid stiffness of our lady Pedro Gorino held to her course and would not give an inch but instead gained to windward and mounted the waves like a Guinea goose. . . .

The tray was lined with green velvet and on its surface as thickly scattered as dewdrops on a field of clover were fifteen or sixteen hundred, purest water diamonds.

There can be little doubt concerning the value of my old friend's contribution. If the book is not just what we expected, I have only myself to blame.

STERLING NORTH

CHICAGO, *July*, 1928

CONTENTS

BOOK I
I GO TO SEA AT THE AGE OF TWELVE

BOOK II
THE PEDRO GORINO

BOOK III
SEGOW FAKU, KING OF THE PONDOS

CONTENTS

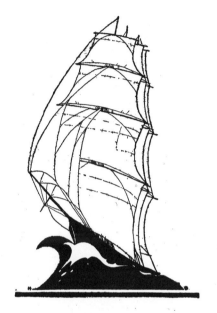

THE PEDRO GORINO

. .
.

BOOK I
I GO TO SEA AT THE AGE OF TWELVE

THE PEDRO GORINO

. .
.

CHAPTER I

MY ANCESTORS WERE SEAFARING MEN

IN the year 1737, when the Atlantic Ocean and the Mediterranean Sea were infested by pirates, there was a pirate ship wrecked off the northwest coast of Africa near the Rio de Oro and all the crew were lost save the captain. McKinnon Paige, the only survivor, owed his life to a young native, Said Kafu, who with the assistance of his people cared for the captain many weeks. After the recovery of Paige, when he had devised a plan whereby he could recover some of the treasure he had buried in Madeira, he induced the young native who had saved his life to accompany him. This boy, being of an adventurous nature with a great desire to see the world, readily accepted and accompanied the pirate to Funchal, Madeira, where they recovered the buried doubloons and sovereigns.

The town itself was quiet, with picturesque streets, a great fort, monasteries, and churches that had been built before the time of Columbus. As Said Kafu wrote many years later, 'With such verdure and bright weather as one may find at Funchal, is it great wonder that even the Roman patricians were constantly voyaging thither?' Women were busy with their lace, while the men made wine from the grapes harvested in the vineyards that covered the steep slopes of the island. One would scarcely realize that this place was the rendezvous of pirates. However, five hundred feet below, down the steep streets leading to the bay, one might have seen a motley crew from all nations.

In that dirty, wild, lively, crescent bay were ships of every variety for here was free port and free anchorage.

McKinnon Paige was a Scotchman and crafty as a fox. He knew his danger now he had no ship. Some few people knew him and among them were men who would have betrayed him. He and the boy haunted the dens along the water-front seeking passage to England. They carried their swords at their sides, for there were feuds among some of the grandees of Funchal often rekindled in the resorts of the seamen. They might have been delayed some weeks had not Paige luckily run across an old mate who had given up the pirate business to become an operator of ships. When at last they were aboard ship, ploughing northward through the rough Atlantic, they were able to draw breath easily again.

The ship stopped at Oporto to take on a cargo of port wine, then up anchor and was on its way again. Crossing the Bay of Biscay a storm arose. Ships were badly made in those days, and the one on which Paige and Said Kafu had taken passage tossed and pitched, creaking in every joint. They weathered the storm, however, and in due time entered the channel. Until they reached the Thames there was little to see except the numerous sailing vessels. Once, at the mouth of the Thames, they took a pilot and made their way through the bustling life up to within three miles of London.

McKinnon Paige was a pirate, but a gentleman. He was devoted to Said Kafu and never deserted the trust. He was grateful to the boy for having saved his life, and in the years of their friendship that followed he never once betrayed him.

Paige changed his name to Slocum, Captain Slocum. He changed the boy's to Sam Cuffee. The pirate's bravado air, fine clothes, silver buckles, and liberal wealth cut a swath with English society. Many a lovely girl, seeing him on the streets of London or at the gala occasions, fell in love with him. The slim Mandingo boy attired in the finest Arabian costume accompanied the pirate and added not a little to the glamour and mystery. Sam Cuffee had learned only a few words of English, but his erect bearing and great devotion to Captain Slocum made the two an object of attention wherever they went.

Whether or not Slocum was in real danger is a question. Certainly he had heard rumors that his real identity was known, and, being fearful for his life and the life of the boy, he planned to flee England. They packed their clothes and their gold in a big sea chest and took passage for the American Colonies. In the spring of the year 1740, they landed at Salem, Massachusetts.

The creeks were running. The cherry and apple orchards covered the hilly countryside with bloom. On the rocky coasts and along the narrow sand beaches the rollers from old storms spent their last force.

Captain Slocum and Sam Cuffee liked the country well. The older man thought it would be profitable to start a ship chandler's outfit and sell to the many vessels coming to port everything that can make a ship seaworthy. So they settled farther down the coast at New Bedford and opened shop. Slocum was a roving spirit. He was continually on the go, aboard some whaler or coastwise freighter. It was his very life. But Sam Cuffee, partner in the new business, stayed conscientiously at home on the job.

Slocum was a gentleman and a scholar. Once free from the pirate life, he never went back. He became an important and respectable New-Englander. His keen eye for business never led him into cheating his customers. During the winter months, when he was not so anxious to be on the sea and business at New Bedford was slow, he spent many hours with Sam Cuffee teaching him all the arts and sciences he knew. When the boy was old enough to have a wife, the old pirate was equal to the occasion. He had seen a fine young 'negro' girl of the Kabyle tribe farther down the New England coast, and he brought her home with him one day aboard his ship. Sam and the girl fell in love at this first meeting and before the spring had passed the two were married.

Captain Slocum had been a true friend. Although he could have sold Sam into slavery anywhere in New England, he never did. Instead he not only had made the boy his partner, educated him, and found him a wife, but now that Sam was married and it was even more important to keep him safe, he bought land on the island of Cuttyhunk and gave it to the young couple. He once wrote of the boy, 'He's a fine lad, aye, bright as a sovereign.'

The pirate, being a Scotchman, was an expert ship-builder. He conceived the idea of starting a small shipyard at Cuttyhunk and he and Sam went to work on their new project. They took great pride in their craft and the ships they built went out to every port in the world. It was in these days that a new type of ship, the schooner, was being evolved on the American coast. The little shipyard worked early and late on orders of the new type. When their first schooner was launched they felt a just pride. From slim masts and new white canvas to oaken keel the boat was all they had dreamed it would be.

During their career as shipbuilders they made several important innovations in rigging. Most of the changes were toward greater simplicity. They experimented with the bowsprit making many delicate adjustments. They improved the system of shrouding a vessel. Their method of stabilizing craft was a contribution to the science of the day.

There on the cold, wave-swept, New England island, Sam Cuffee and his young wife raised their family. Four boys and ten girls were born to the pair. The boys grew up to help their father with his business in his older years. The girls married into free 'negro' families along the coast. But these children were born into a world that misunderstood their position in life and treated them with a disrespect that was not their due. Maritime people are aristocrats wherever they go. The discipline and training of the sea endows men with unquenchable courage, and these free New England 'negroes' were as fearless seamen and as aristocratic in bearing as any Nordic you may offer.

In the year 1772 Sam Cuffee died of pneumonia. Paul, his fourth and youngest son, then but thirteen years of age, was to carry his father's name proudly to many countries. As the boy grew, he felt more and more strongly the unjust prejudice against his race. There were no public schools where he could obtain an education, and because of his color he was barred from the private schools. Consequently he educated himself.

When he grew to be a man, the thought of his bitter youth still rankled within him and he decided that as far as it was within his power he would make it easier for the children of the next generation. About the year 1781 he set the example for Massachusetts by building a public school at his own expense on Cutty-hunk Island and inviting all children both colored and white to attend. They came from as far as New Brunswick on the north and New York on the south.

Like his father, Paul was a shipbuilder. One of his dreams was to build a ship faster than any on the Atlantic. All his ability went into designing the Traveler and she was one of the fastest sailing ships afloat. Officially she was a brig, but the genius of Captain Paul Cuffee gave her a unique and elaborate rigging.

On every boat he commanded he taught the crew all the arts and sciences he knew. A great part of his life was spent trying to help those who had not had his opportunities.

But, although he was a friend to those who would be his friends, he was a splendid warrior when he sensed intolerance. On one occasion early in his life when he found that because of his color he was not to be allowed to vote, he refused to pay his taxes; and because of the principle at stake, stubbornly continued to refuse until he was at last thrown into prison. Paul Cuffee was the first 'negro' to petition the powers that be in regard to slavery. His document was addressed to the Legislature of New Jersey asking that body to petition the Congress of the United States that every slave be freed and that every colored man that so desired be allowed to leave America. This petition was one of the first bits of motivation in a controversy which still rages. It subsequently led to the founding of the American Colonization Society.

Before the War of 1812 he had outfitted his brig the Traveler, and sailed it to Norway, Russia, Denmark, England, and France. He had circumnavigated Africa, investigating its shores to discover the best place to found a national home for freed slaves. Having finally decided on the Cape of Good Hope, he returned to England where he obtained the coöperation and enthusiastic assistance of Bishop Wilberforce, Clarkson the great abolitionist, the Duke of Portland, and several other noblemen.

These humanitarians arranged to secure the means to pay the southern planters the price of their slaves. The coöperation of the British Government was obtained whereby they were to purchase the British Territory of the Cape of Good Hope. Paul was to transport those who would be free to their new national home. But the slavers and the pro-slave element in England, America, France, Spain, Portugal, and the Islands were sufficiently strong to defeat the great 'negro' both at home and abroad.

When the War of 1812 broke out, Paul Cuffee was again on the sea. He was encountered by an English gunboat. Since his brig was unarmed and the sea was crowded with his enemies, he thought it best to submit peacefully to arrest. When he was brought into port, Wilberforce and others heard of his plight and had him released.

Only a few weeks later through the machinations of the Americans, who hated him, he was again arrested, this time by ships of his own Government. Had he not been a friend of President Madison, his ship might have been tied up indefinitely. Madison knew Cuffee's quest, however, and was able to secure his release.

It was during these harassing days that Cuffee decided to hit the first physical blow at slavery. From all along the Atlantic seaboard he gathered a little band of free 'negroes' who were with him heart and soul in his colonization project. He then dropped anchor in New York Harbor, armed and provisioned his boat and prepared for a bolder stroke.

The mother of John Kinsell, one of the boys in his crew, was a slave on a South Carolina plantation. Cuffee determined to free her, and slipped southward for that purpose. When they had anchored off the Carolina shore, he decided to free not only the mother of John Kinsell, but every slave on the plantation. Leading his crew of eighteen huskies ashore, he freed the overjoyed slaves, burned their miserable huts, and put to sea. The glow from the fires shone on the dark water. By morning they were far out on the Atlantic.

The Traveler headed straight for West Africa and made the trip in record time. There were, besides the captain and crew, twelve slaves taken from the plantation and the free 'negroes' he had picked up along the coast. He landed them on the coast of Sierra Leone at Free Town, West Africa. Paul Cuffee had given these people all he had. It was necessary to go to England for funds and provisions. Consequently he left the colony in the hands of John Kinsell and Frank James and sailed northward. But Governor McCarthy, Governor of Sierra Leone, was as heartless as many of his successors, a true imperialist. He drove these people away. They would have perished, but were rescued by Lieutenant Stockton, of the United States Navy, who assisted them down the coast to a little island in the mouth of the Monsarada River, where they founded the colony that later became the Republic of Liberia.

Meanwhile the sisters and brothers of Paul Cuffee had scattered all over the world. Paul himself, having married a girl in New Bedford, had raised a family of three girls and four boys.

His youngest son, John Cuffee, like his father and grandfather, was well educated. On June 5, 1817, a letter directed to Paul Cuffee asked the old captain his advice in the choice of a school teacher for a secret school for 'negro' children to be founded in Charleston, South Carolina. Cuffee realized the great danger but sent his son John. The older man knew the boy might be apprehended anywhere along the way, tried and sold into slavery, but his heart was with his race and he told the boy to go.

In attempting to get to his destination via the underground railroad John was betrayed.

He sent this short letter to his father:

YORK JAIL, *January* 13, 1818

DEAR FATHER,

This is to inform thee that in my journey to Alexandria I have been apprehended and confined in prison for an Imposter, they say I am not your son and for that reason I wish thee come on immediately or send some of the Neighbors, and by that means I can get released from this place, the two men that had me taken are named Jonathan Jessup and Amos Gilbert two friends both residing in this place, they say that I must prove that I am thy Son or else I must stand trial at the next court which is April ———

this from thy Son

JOHN CUFFEE

the name of the place is little York Pennsylvania About 90 miles from Philadelphia.

The letter must have reached Paul Cuffee as he was dying. Help was slow in coming and John was in jail many weeks. It is unknown how he escaped, but one of his later letters tells how he hid days and traveled nights, finally arriving at Marietta, Ohio. Here he was given asylum by a group of abolitionists.

This was dreamy country. He had been promised safety, and the fertile fields, lush meadows and gently rolling country all held him with their spell. He forgot his goal in South Carolina as any other boy of twenty might have done. Only occasionally did he think of the sea and the wild New England coast.

Soon he married and took a little farm. To John Cuffee and his wife was born one child, Susan Cuffee, great-grand-daughter of Sam Cuffee. She was a mild-natured little girl, fond of her books and the quiet life about their home. When she grew up she married a

Mr. Shepherd, who took her to live with him in Lancaster, Pennsylvania. He died shortly leaving her with one child. Here she met John Dean, son of a wealthy Philadelphia merchant, who fell in love with her. They were married and went to live in Philadelphia. John Dean's family had come from Quata, Morocco. For three generations they had been wealthy merchants of Philadelphia. During colonial times they were under the protection of the British and Portuguese Governments and after the United States became a free country they continued in their business.

Of this union of Susan Cuffee and John Dean, I, Captain Harry Dean, was born, November 20, 1864.

CHAPTER II

I GO TO SEA

THERE were eighteen children in my family, seven boys and eleven girls. I was the youngest boy. Of that family only three of us are now alive, Alice, Mayme, and I.

I am an African and proud of it. There is not a drop of white blood in my veins. My ancestors have been sea captains and merchants and I have spent my life on the sea.

My father was a tall, proud, not very religious, but kindly sort of man. My mother was a fine singer and a cultured and idealistic woman. I hope I have proved worthy of them.

While I was still a boy I was given copies of Horace, Homer, Virgil, Petrarch, Shakespeare, Coleridge's 'Ancient Mariner,' a translation of 'The Arabian Chronicles,' 'Arabian Nights,' Colonel George Williams's 'History of the Negro,' a hand-illumined 'Spirit of the Laws,' and many others. Mother delighted in training us, and when I was old enough she put me under the tutelage of Fannie Jackson, the great 'negro' woman educator, at the Institute for Colored Youth in Philadelphia. Here I was taught grammar, arithmetic, and a foundation in the five natural sciences. Everything theoretical, nothing practical.

I lived such a sheltered life that I became idealistic. I was entirely unaware of the race problem. I knew nothing of the hardships and treacheries of life. We had all the money we needed and I knew nothing of poverty. Since that time I have experienced all the hardships known to man.

Often we had visitors. Major Martin R. Delaney, major in the Union Army during the Civil War; United States Senator Revels; and General Belaski, an escaped rebel officer from Cuba, were among the most frequent. I remember General Belaski in particular. He was as black as pitch and as far across as he was tall. He told me stories of the Cuban Rebellion in his mild voice. 'I come from salt water, Sonny, land alive! Should see them islands and the sea a-swishin' on the shore. Should see them black boys, Sonny, creepin' on their bellies through the brush. Guns no good, clothes all ragged, but filled with the spirit and not afraid o' the Devil hisself.' It was music to my young ears. I could have listened forever.

Besides these few celebrities there were many fine neighbors, particularly the Mintons, Wares, Fortunes, and Dutrelles, a strange class of people whose history has never been written. They were for the most part of maritime ancestors and had become enmeshed in the devastating American environment only after generations of protest. We kept in close contact with these people, for they were the few who could understand our aims and ideals.

The summer I was twelve we went as usual to our cottage at Atlantic City. I swam in the sea and played on the beaches in the sunshine. Some days my father would let me ride in the little twenty-ton schooners whose business it was to carry any who chose to the horizon and back for twenty-five cents. Suddenly I was crazy to go to sea. The salty tang in the air, the rough sailors, the glamour about boats, the stories of adventure I had heard all through my childhood, filled me with a tremendous urge. I thought of the sea night and day.

On returning to Philadelphia we found my Uncle Silas, an honest-to-goodness sea captain come to stay with us for a few days. He was preparing to make a three-year voyage around the world, aboard his ship Traveler the Second. He was, therefore, a hero. He was a man of splendid physique, rapid in his movements and a true sea captain. He had a terrible stare. I was never sure when he looked at me whether he was angry or not. If he had not been my uncle I should have been afraid of him. But his stories were as rich and fabulous as those of Sinbad the Sailor.

One evening as we sat at supper he said to my father: 'John, I can tell by the cut of his jib the boy would make a good sailor. He'd reef and furl in no time and I'd have him boxing the compass and shooting the sun before we got around the Horn. Why not let me take him along?'

It seemed as if whole minutes passed before my father answered and when he did I hung on every word.

'Would you take good care of him, Silas?'

'Bring him back shipshape or my name's not Dean,' my uncle answered.

'The sea's a rough place for a boy.'

'There's nothing like the sea to test what's in a boy. It would make a man of him, John.'

'I'll have to think it out,' my father said. 'Give me

till morning.' He seemed worried that evening. Mother cried a little. But with all the thoughtlessness of youth I was hardly aware of their sorrow. It was more miraculous than my Arabian Nights. They must let me go, I knew they would. But why did I have to wait until morning to be sure? My brain was whirling with excitement and emotion.

Morning came at last. I could go. Ah, Christophe, Toussaint l'Ouverture, strong men of my race, were you as exultant in your power as I in mine upon that happy morning! In my imagination I already ruled the seas. I had a fleet of ships, their white sails filled with the wind. But little did I realize the hardships of the sea or the hard life that awaited me. And little did I realize the impotence of a child of twelve.

My uncle and I took a train from Philadelphia and landed at Jersey City late at night. We went from the station to the ferry landing and for the first time I saw the lights of New York. The way they were reflected on the dark waters of the Hudson stays with me all these years. Then aboard the ferry boat. Everywhere there was the bustle of boats, horns blowing, and men calling over the water. Having lived in the quiet city of Philadelphia all my life, I had never seen anything like this wild, tumultuous life. We landed at wooden docks that thronged with rough dirty barefoot boys selling newspapers, sleeping in out-of-the-way corners, fighting for no apparent reason. It was an Irish part of town crowded with sailors and toughs. Uncle Silas pushed and crowded, pulling me along by the hand. We passed along narrow streets and between high brick buildings until we came to Manetta Lane, squalid enough to-day but respectable then. Here we put up for the night with an aunt who made a great fuss over me. 'Honey-chile let me give yo' one mo' cake.'

The next morning we went down to the harbor and for the first time I saw my uncle's ship, Traveler the Second. I liked the smell of Stockholm tar. The way the sailing vessels floated and bobbed on the water was a mystery. The lines and the rigging of the ship impressed me and set me wondering. I remember the Traveler was a barkentine with both square rig and fore-and-aft rig, a mixture of the two types of rigging. She carried studding booms for studding sails that bellied balloon-like on each side so that to those on board and to those who saw her pass, she gave the impression of a sea-gull on the wing. She was very fast under full sail.

There on the docks at New York were sailors from every country. Some of them were dressed in flannel shirts as red as fire. Their great bulging muscles showed through their clothing. Where their sleeves were rolled up their strong brown arms rippled like the surface of water in a breeze. The proportions of these men and their hoarse voices impressed me and made me wish I were as big and strong as they.

Where will you find such men now? Gone are the sailing vessels and gone the men who sailed them. They were a singing, laughing, bunch in port, but let their ship get into rough weather rounding the Horn or off the Cape of Storms, up in the Gulf of Alaska or wherever they were, let the decks get icy and the gale go whistling and moaning through the shrouds, and see if they weren't as true as steel. No grumbling or growling when the bos'n called 'All hands ahoy!' They're gone now, but there they were on the dock at New York and aboard the Traveler when I went to sea as a boy.

Sometimes chanties came clearly over the water, one sailor singing a line, the crew answering:

> 'Haul the bowline, the good ship's a rolling.
> Haul the bowline, the bowline haul.'

Then before I could catch more, a dozen voices on the dock laughing and shouting would drown out the singing. 'Give a hand there, man.'

'An' if the mate ain't seven kinds of Devil I ain't never been in Cork.'

'Shet your mouth, Folley. Give a heave on that puncheon.'

'Where's Mr. Watson? Oh, Mr. Watson.'

It was our men making the racket. They were loading the cargo of hardware, notions, bright cloth, beads and trade goods of all kinds into puncheons, great barrel-like containers as tall as a man. They had been at the work for over a week. The Traveler had made her departure from Boston some two weeks before, dropped anchor at New York and prepared to receive cargo. Uncle Silas had come to Philadelphia to get me, leaving the loading of the vessel in charge of the first mate. We had arrived in New York in time to see the last of that work.

My uncle was talking to the first mate. 'We'll muster the men this evening, Mr. Watson. See that they're aboard early. We'll up anchor at dawn.' My uncle and I went aboard late that afternoon and made ourselves comfortable in his spacious cabin. What a great man I thought him, with his charts, and sextants, and compasses, his wealth of sea knowledge, and his exciting stories. Aboard ship, however, he had little time to play. His stern expression seldom relaxed into a smile. And although I admired and respected him as did his sailors, I was a little in awe of this dark brown giant whose word was law to so many men. And he was a man to inspire awe, courageous, as every sea captain must be. I found in the days that followed that he was perfectly fearless and would never shorten sail until the decks were at an angle of forty degrees.

At dawn we made our departure from Red Bank. We might have been a phantom ship we moved so gently over the ocean. The pale early morning light flooded the decks of the ship where men moving at their work seemed scarcely men of this world. But as the breeze stiffened and the sun rose higher and the last mist of sleep cleared from before my eyes, I realized that we had put to sea and that my life of adventure had begun. Because of my experiences on the small pleasure schooners I felt myself quite a sailor. The commodious barkentine seemed perfectly safe in my young eyes. Everything was expectation. I wanted to see pirates and buried treasure. I wanted to lead a wild and gallant life. I did not realize how helpless I was or how unprepared for the sea and the hardships of sailors.

The crew was a mixed one. More than half of the men were 'negroes.' As they worked they sang,

'For seven long years I courted Sally,
Weigh, roll and go.

The sweetest flower in all the valley;
Spend my money on Sally Brown.'

How many times I was to hear that and similar songs, filled with the wailing rhythm of the African race. What is it you have lost, what have you left behind, what are you looking for, you unhappy hostages of an alien race?

At Charleston, South Carolina, a colored pilot came out in a small sailing vessel and took us into port. That was the only colored pilot I ever saw in American waters. I remember my uncle had a lot of trouble in Charleston. There was an argument with a port official of which I caught but little and understood less.

'Ain't no nigguh goin' run this po't,' the official shouted.

And my uncle in his quiet cold voice, 'I merely asked for clearance papers and the usual civility shown a ship's officer.'

Whatever the trouble was, my uncle thought it necessary to admonish the crew not to leave the ship. He told them that the boat was to up anchor the minute the clearance papers were ready. Other crews swarmed all along the water-front, but ours remained aboard the ship sullen and angry. Each man felt that the indignity done the ship was a personal affront.

My uncle and I went ashore, however. I accompanied him everywhere, particularly to the custom house. We were in Charleston over one Sunday. We went to church. The colored people were nice to us, but their dialect was so strange that I could scarcely understand them at times.

At last we got our clearance papers and made our departure. We were no sooner out of the harbor than we ran into severe rain and hail storms. The ship was fighting adverse winds and currents and the hail set up a great tattoo on the deck. I was too young to realize our danger. The excitement was more or less pleasurable to me. That night was an anxious one for the crew and for my uncle.

I could not understand the serious demeanor of the men. None of them would talk or laugh with me. Each hurried about the deck doing his appointed task. Some clambered up the ratlines to reef sails, some pulled and hauled on halyards. The mate's orders and the crew's 'Aye, aye, sir!' were carried far out over the water by the storm. I heard their voices as if they had come from a great distance.

Most of the crew were on deck all night. And although my uncle told me to go to my bunk in the cabin and get some sleep I was unable to close my eyes. I was not afraid. But I was aware of a sinister foreboding. It was as if the sailors could sense something terrible and strange, something within the darkness which I could not see or hear or feel with my unaccustomed senses. Of course the weather was dark and stormy with black clouds hurrying across the flattened dome of heaven, but that alone was not enough to account for their actions. Their silence was more expressive than all the rough weather.

Later in the night the rain and hail let up and I got out of my bunk to see how things were going on deck. At the door of the galley sat Johnson, a fine old man who was our cook and steward. He liked me a great deal and always carried on an engaging conversation. Even he was still. He had been sitting there at the door of his galley all night. His pipe had long since gone out. When I spoke to him he would only answer in monosyllables. The sea was running high and white caps were breaking. The salt spray stung my face. And although I did not realize that we were on a lee shore with a shifting wind and in great danger, I did know that I was lonesome and lost and very homesick.

CHAPTER III
WE ROUND THE HORN

THE next morning the fog was so thick that we ran into one another on the deck. I bumped against the sailors moving about their work. The air was gradually warming which was pleasing to me as the night had been chilly. My uncle's voice boomed through the fog, 'Square the main foresail.'

From everywhere about me the crew answered, 'Aye, aye, the main foresail.'

My uncle kept telling the crew to put up this sail and that sail until we were nothing but a mass of white sails. I do not know how long the fog lasted but soon the sun was shining and we were bowling along. We came without mishap to St. Augustine and there we dropped anchor.

This town was more quaint than any I had ever seen, old and picturesque. The thing that struck me was the sunlight on the old plaster buildings and the planes of light and shadow. That impression stays with me although much else is forgotten. It was fifty years ago when I was but a boy and the trip is like a dream.

I remember we left the ship in the harbor at St. Augustine and went overland to Jacksonville. My uncle wished to see several friends and do business there. I had never seen so many colored people. I remember the St. John's River at Jacksonville. It was not until I visited the west coast of Africa that I saw anything to surpass it.

The next day we went aboard the ship at St. Augustine and made our departure. A stiff breeze carried us southward along the coast of Florida. Most of the time we were within sight of the sandy beach that looked in the bright sunlight like a white ribbon. At four bells in the morning a few days later, we came into the Gulf of Mexico and I saw that body of water for the first time. The mate who was a Yankee took a great delight in fishing. When we sailed into the Gulf he took out his fish lines and began fishing off the taffrail. As he fished he sang,

'So let the waves go rolling,
And let the wind go blow;
A sailor man's a free man
As only sailors know . . .'

He stopped abruptly seeing me approach fish line in hand. He asked me in his gruff voice, 'Sonny, what you fishin' for — whale?' Then he laughed a great laugh and went to singing again, hardly waiting for my answer, beginning his song where he had left off,

'The town is neat and handy
For girls and gaiety
But life is worth the living
On the wide blue sea.'

He paid no attention to me at all, but continued to smoke and fish, occasionally bursting into song in his thunderous voice.

I was not to be discouraged, however. After throwing out my line I stood looking at the wake of the boat and wondering what happened to waves when they disappeared and wondering how it was that after a boat had gone by, the water got smooth again so that you could not even see where it passed. Suddenly the line was almost jerked from my hands. I hung on with all my strength and was almost pulled over the taffrail. I was so startled that I had no idea for a moment what had happened. I braced myself against the rail and called loudly for help. The mate and others came to my assistance and heaved away on the line. As they pulled a great fish jumped out of the water. The sun struck his scales, making a gleaming silver halo about him.

'Shiver my timbers if he ain't a silver king!' said the mate, his voice betraying both admiration and envy. We pulled him aboard. He was a beauty and weighed a little over seventy-five pounds. I was very proud. He was cooked for dinner, and the steward, old Johnson, gave me the first choice of the meat. It was the most delicious fish I have ever tasted.

The weather was clear on the Gulf. The water was as blue as indigo, shading to green. The sky curved over us like a silver bell. When I went on deck each morning I could hardly believe my senses. I did not want to take time to eat or sleep. I wanted to be everywhere all the time, seeing everything, doing everything, and missing nothing.

The crew was a big one and there was plenty of help. The watches were regular. There were none ill aboard ship at this time. The sailors were busy splicing ropes, making knots, weaving mats, carving ship models and doing the thousand and one things sailors do in good weather. One man was painting pictures of the sea, and of the ports we visited. Folley, an Irish-American with a slight brogue, was making corn-cob pipes. Like the rest of the crew he wanted to teach me his handicraft. 'I'll show ye how to make a pipe as would satisfy the King o' England hisself, the bloody rascal. Here, hold your knife so. Scrape her smooth. When you get through doin' that you cut a little hole for the stem, so. There, yer catchin' on. You'll be making better pipes than old Folley hisself 'fore we get around the Horn.' And then when the lesson was over he would say, 'Sure an' you'll be a divil with the girls one o' these fine days. There's fine brown girls in every port as will be fallin' all over thimselves makin' eyes at ye. The best part o' goin' to sea is agoin' ashore on pay day. But you're too young a lad to be thinkin' on thim things.'

When we arrived at the mouth of the Mississippi River, we beat about for several hours waiting for a pilot. It was early morning and as the sun came higher and higher we could see where the muddy water of the river hit the blue water of the Gulf. When the pilot finally came aboard he took us to anchor near a bank overlooking a marshy flat. There were thousands of wild ducks and geese on the marsh. Some of them flew nearly over us, making a sharp whistling sound with their wings.

We hitched to a tug later in the day. It pulled us off up the river toward New Orleans. We passed two forts that the sailors seemed to know about. This started tales of bloodshed and heroism as some of the men had fought in the Civil War and were very bitter about it. Farther up the river we saw an encampment of men, probably a gang working on the levee. The war stories told by the sailors had excited my imagination to the point where I believed these gangs of workmen were rebel soldiers and that our ship the Traveler was a Union gunboat. The imaginary battle carried with it all the thrill of siege and all the glamour of victory.

As we went on up the river the shores became greener. The trees had streamers of moss hanging from their branches. It was my first introduction to the subtropics and the flora was unlike any I had known.

When we finally got up to New Orleans we went through locks into the heart of the city. What an attractive and busy place it was. There were ships and boats of all sorts. Great swarthy sailors ran up and down their decks.

My uncle and I went ashore and after walking a long time we came to a low building where there were thousands of people trading. The many narrow stalls held merchandise of every variety. We stopped while he took care of some business. Then we walked up Canal Street, a street lined with stores and swarming with more kinds of people than I had ever seen. There were brown, black, yellow, and white people all talking in different languages. After my uncle had transacted some business at the custom house we went to my aunt's.

She was a sister of my father and of Uncle Silas. She lived on a street called Elysian Fields. My aunt deserved a street with such a name. She was the kindest little lady I have ever met, and she took a liking to me from the first. Although I was only twelve years old and nowhere near my full growth, my aunt was so short that she only came up to my shoulder. She wore her hair in tight curls all over her head. There were great gold earrings in her pretty brown ears. Her silk skirts stood way out on each side and rustled when she walked. When she went out of doors she put a bright shawl over her head.

She would say, 'Come here, chile. Where'd you get dem big brown eyes? You am most delectable enough to eat. Better stay here with your po' Aunt Sylvia. She'll feed you all de chicken you can eat. This am the Promised Land, chile, the land ob milk and honey. The sharks'll get you if you go to sea. Stay here in Noo Orleans by de big dreamy river.'

We were treated so well in New Orleans that we must have stayed a month or six weeks. We finally had to leave, however. So aboard the Traveler once more, down the river, and out into the Gulf. The weather was warm and dreamy. I lived the life of a young prince. We went down the coast to Galveston, then to Vera Cruz. I had read a book about the Mexicans while I was still a boy and I watched them with interest at Vera Cruz.

If I remember rightly we went to the West Indies next and traveled in and out among the islands trading with the English. I remember we sighted Barbados on our starboard. My uncle told me that somewhere here on the sea-floor lay the bones of Francis Drake, with the fish swimming over and the white sand beneath. Later we dropped anchor at Bridgetown and did some trading.

We took on water at a little island where the people were all colored and all talked like Irishmen which amused us greatly. Several big black fellows came aboard the ship and started chattering in a brogue as broad as you could find in Dublin.

'Sure an' it's a foin ship ye got, Mister Dean. It's been many a day since we've seen the likes of her in these waters.'

Folley was dozing in the forecastle. A half dozen wags went to get him up.

'Wake up, Folley. We just dropped anchor off the Emerald Isle. The skipper he's been fooling us all this time and here we are at Ireland. Your ma and pa is waiting for you on the dock.' Poor Folley followed his tormentors to the deck racking his sleepy brain in a vain effort to get his bearings. For one amazed and bewildered moment he stood and listened to the natives. Then grabbing a belaying pin he shouted, 'Holy Saint Patrick, insult an Irishman, will ye. I'll bust yer bloody heads.'

He would have done it, too, if the mate had not come down just then to see what all the racket was about.

There was one little island, Bocas del Torres, a key some five or six miles long where we stopped for several days. It was covered with banana trees, palms, paw-paws, and guavas. The people fed us the best sweet potatoes I have ever eaten and turtle meat from the turtles caught on the beach of the lagoon. The shells of these turtles were so large that some of the little black boys turned them upside down and used them for boats, paddling all about in the shallow water sitting in the shell. The last day we were on the key was a Sunday and several of us went to church. The next day we made our departure and headed south for Pernambuco, Brazil.

At Pernambuco almost every one was dark, and spoke

Portuguese. The ship's agent here was a busy, excitable little man. He had a great lot of freight to exchange for the goods we had aboard. He would say, 'Jesus! Caramba! Caracoles!' and hurry off down the deck. He and Uncle Silas talked together a great deal in the strange and beautiful language of Spain. In a day or two we made our departure. At Rio de Janeiro and at Santos we sent our freight ashore in lighters and took on coffee.

I shall never forget the five weeks after our departure from Santos. After we had sailed I do not know how many days, the days and nights became more chill. My uncle and the first mate were always talking about adjusting the compass. They figured many hours every day. We had been lightly dressed at Santos but as we approached the Horn it became colder and colder. The weather was consistently bad. Old Johnson began to keep the galley door closed. The ship was put in shape for rough weather. Extra lashing was used here and there; hatches were seen to. Anxious eyes watched the foreboding heavens.

It seemed as though the crew never rested. My uncle was on deck most of the time. He would come into the cabin, his oilskins dripping and his hands numb with cold. But after snatching a half hour's rest he would go on deck again.

The ship was heavily loaded, and although normally she rode the waves like a gull, rising to each ominous gray mountain of water and gliding gracefully into each valley, her cargo was so heavy that sometimes she would plow sullenly into an oncoming wave flooding the decks with rushing water.

I watched the angry sea through a porthole and remembering bits from the 'Ancient Mariner' repeated to myself:

> 'With sloping masts and dipping prow
> As who pursued with yell and blow
> Still treads the shadow of his foe,
> And forward bends his head,
> The ship drove fast, loud roared the blast
> And southward aye we fled.'

I had known winter in Pennsylvania and in New England, but this was much colder. The bitter wind cut us to the bone. It seemed as though we had been transported into another world, this trackless waste of water was so different from anything I had ever known. The sun was always overshadowed and the cold darkness hung about us like a veil hiding the past and the future. We dared not speak, we dared not even let our thoughts go astray. If we opened our mouths at all it was to shout with a fearlessness we did not feel, as if the sound of fierce voices might subdue the elements where no amount of supplication would avail.

Only once was there an interlude. On a day a little brighter than usual we sighted the bare rocky coast of Tierra del Fuego. I was interested in this bleak land. There were birds that the sailors called Cape pigeons here. Twice during the morning we saw an albatross. By noon the oppressing darkness had closed in about us again.

Each time we attempted to round the Horn we were beaten back. The sea was running high and the terrible cross currents, adverse waves, and pitiless wind made us fight for every inch of progress. We were almost stripped but even the few sails we used were continually being reefed and furled. The sailors made their way up the ratlines laboriously and at great danger as every inch of rigging was thick with ice. I would wake a half dozen times in the night and hear the bos'n shouting, 'All hands on deck, ahoy.'

And from far away the weary 'Aye, aye, sir,' of the crew. And I would crawl deeper into my heavy blankets, happy that I did not have to get out and work on the bitter cold deck, or climb out on icy rigging fifty feet above the rushing foaming sea to furl or reef a sail.

The first mate wanted to take advantage of the favorable winds and go east to the west coast of Africa and around the Cape of Good Hope. But my uncle was a determined man. He said we had started west and west we would go. For three terrible weeks we tossed and pitched and beat about. At last on our third attempt we got around the Horn, and with great thanksgiving moved northward along the west coast of South America.

CHAPTER IV

OUT TO THE SANDWICH ISLANDS,
BACK TO THE BARBARY COAST

THE weather grew steadily better and better. We felt as though we could never get enough of the warm sunshine flooding the deck. Soon the dampness, which had made our life miserable for the past month, left the cabin and the forecastle. The cook threw wide the galley door. Warm winds carried us northward over a gently rolling sea.

My uncle started to teach me what he knew about the stars. The deck was pleasantly cool in the evening. We would go out toward the end of the second dog-watch, about eight o'clock, and stay until almost midnight. I learned to know Orion, the Pleiades, Rigel, the Southern Cross, and many others. But the stars that stirred my imagination most were those in Cepheus, Cepheus, King of Ethiopia. Sometimes the stars seemed infinitely distant and aloof. But as we came into lower latitudes, they became softly luminous and seemed near enough to touch the tips of the masts. Sometimes I could imagine they were enmeshed in the shrouds.

Finally we came to Lima, Peru, and dropped anchor. There was a big Peruvian warship in the harbor with some such name as the Hawaskai. My uncle was a good friend of her captain. The Peruvian was a tall dark-skinned man, a Spanish type; a descendant of the Spanish adventurers who conquered the Incas and stole their gold. At his invitation we went aboard his ship. I marveled at the guns and at the massive construction.

A few days later we made our departure and set sail for the Sandwich Islands. We sailed day after day over a sea so hot and glaring that it might have been molten metal. Twice we were becalmed and the ship lay like a tired bird on the glassy water. Finally one morning we heard from aloft the welcome cry of 'Land ahoy.'

Then some one struck up the chanty so often sung when the ship makes landfall:

> 'Only one more day a-reefing,
> One more day;
> Oh, rock and roll me over,
> Only one more day.'

In due time we dropped anchor at Honolulu and went ashore. Here my uncle knew King Kalakaua. He was a full-blooded king. His skin was dark brown and he had very large brown eyes. He was fat and jovial and everybody liked him. My uncle and the King had a great old bout on champagne. I was allowed to come along, but all they let me have were unfermented drinks. The three of us, together with the King's retinue, went from store to store and saloon to saloon all over the city of Honolulu. The King kept telling everybody who my uncle was and what a fine fellow he had turned out to be. The King carried a bottle with him as an extra precaution against the long thirsty voyages between saloons. What a time we had wandering about arm in arm and singing the greatest songs. When we got tired we lay right down in the middle of the road in the good old dirt. Then somebody would think of a place we had not visited. Up we would get and off we would go, fully determined that while there were new worlds to conquer we would not lay down our armor.

We hated to leave Honolulu, but all good things must come to an end. King Kalakaua and his retinue came down to the docks to bid us good-bye. He looked so dejected that my uncle promised to visit him the very next time he was on the Pacific. They had a drink on that and parted happy.

We almost doubled on our tracks and headed for the Bay of Banderas in Mexico. We had an uneventful trip. The sea was smooth enough and there was a good breeze.

My friend the bos'n, whose name was Washington, would have done anything in the world for me. He was short and black and very pleasant. Although he was little taller than I, he had massive shoulders. He was as quick as a cat. There were men aboard the ship twice as big as he and as strong as lions, but not one would have fought the bos'n. When any two of the crew got to quarreling he would walk up to him and say, 'Listen, black boys, better stop yer dickering. That ain't no way for two shipmates to act. Make you fight it out if you don't stop yer fooling. And the winner has to answer to the bos'n, Mr. Washington, who can lick the tar out o' any man aboard.' That would quiet them down. Sometimes when the men would get too boisterous in the forecastle he would shout down with his gruff voice, 'Ahoy down there! Where's yer manners? I ain't going to tolerate no ruction in the fo'-castle.'

Not all the men aboard were as even-tempered as the

bos'n. They were, however, the most gentlemanly crew I have ever met. Despite the fact it was a mixed crew there were seldom any hard feelings. There was not a lubber or a mope among them. They were the only crew in all my sea experience who addressed each other as 'Mister.' There was not as much complaining about the food as one generally finds aboard ship.

We bowled along day after day and at length reached the Bay of Banderas on the coast of Mexico. As our water was very low we took on a fresh supply. We also did some trading with the Mexicans. After several days my uncle gave the order to up anchor and we made our departure bound for Santa Barbara, California. As we sailed northward we were at times within sight of the shore where we could see the surf bursting against the rocks or sweeping far up onto the sandy beaches. At last we came to Santa Barbara. We had no sooner dropped anchor than we saw a coastwise, side-wheel steamer filled with passengers come up to the wharf. The whole town flocked down to meet it. The women wore wonderfully colored dresses and bright mantillas. The men wore boots with high heels, bright silk handkerchiefs around their necks, leather belts studded with brass and silver, and high sombreros. The crowd floated down the hill bright as petals from jungle flowers. We went ashore and saw the old Spanish mission. Everywhere there were Mexicans, weaving blankets.

We made our departure the next morning as my uncle was anxious to reach San Francisco. Our journey was without mishap and we sighted the Golden Gate late one afternoon with the setting sun shining upon it. Somehow it seemed we were about to enter the opening in a high wall. It might have been the gate to Heaven, the abutments were so massive and golden. I half expected it to shut with a sound like thunder, denying us entrance. We beat about for some time. When the pilot boat finally arrived, who should come aboard but my Uncle Solomon, who was the ship's agent at San Francisco. This was my first meeting with Uncle Solomon, although I had heard so much about his exciting life on the sea that I felt as though I knew him. He was white-haired but hearty. He still kept his sea legs. My uncles had not seen each other for several years. They shook hands quietly, these two brothers who had so much in common yet so little to say. They had fought side by side in every part of the world and weathered many storms together. They did not talk of their adventures now. They sat together at the break of the poop looking out over the bay, as if silence were more expressive than any words could be.

Finally Uncle Solomon said, 'We're getting too old for the sea.'

'Aye, we are.'

'Been a couple of sea tramps, Silas, a couple of sailors as would cry at the sight of land; but those days are gone.'

'They're gone, Solomon.'

'And what will come of the Deans when we're dead, and not a skipper among them?'

'I've been thinking of that these ten years, Solomon. And I've thought it out. That's why I took this boy aboard. He'll make a sea captain or I don't know men.'

I had been listening up to this time, but something about their words troubled me and I moved away. It was as though I were suddenly burdened with a great responsibility. It seemed that all my seafaring ancestors were watching me from their graves on the land and in the dark sea, trying to determine if their faith had been misplaced.

My two uncles went ashore and got permanent anchorage from the port captain. We anchored far down the bay below Alameda. A few of the men were crazy to be ashore. Folley in particular could scarcely wait to see the Barbary Coast again. And some of the men had sweethearts in San Francisco.

> 'Sally Brown was a Creole lady,
> Weigh, aye, roll and go,
> Sally Brown was a Creole lady,
> Spend my money on Sally Brown.'

I had heard so much about the Barbary Coast from the sailors that I wanted to see it for myself. I asked my uncle to take me ashore so that I might see it. He said it was no place for little boys. However I finally had my way.

The Barbary Coast at this time was about the toughest place on earth. When gold was discovered in California, all the pirates, high-jackers, ex-slavers, and cut-throats in the world flocked to San Francisco. There were still a good many when I was there. Everywhere north of what is now Montgomery Avenue and Washington Street were low wooden buildings. There were dance halls, gambling places, and little gymnasiums for wrestlers and prize fighters. I remember there were painted women in all the dance halls. Every time a sailor or miner came in the door, one of them would take him by the arm.

This was the last stand of the frontier. The miners from back in the mountains came down to throw away their gold. When I was there back in the seventies they were still carrying gold dust in pouches and paying for their drinks with the dust. They wore high boots, red shirts, bandannas around their necks, and great felt hats. They were romantic-looking fellows in their picturesque garb.

We went ashore to see the Barbary Coast and ate at a French restaurant a few blocks from the district. We had a seven-course meal with wine. The food was excellent.

We met Folley at one of the saloons. He was ugly drunk. 'Better go aboard ship,' my uncle told him.

'Say, Skipper, ain't this shore leave we're on? I'll not go aboard this night, so help me, damned if I will.'

'Have your own way,' my uncle said, as we were walking away. 'But you'll be in trouble before the evening is over. You're in a tough crowd.'

'These here lubbers,' he shouted after us. 'I kin lick ten o' thim sober and twenty when I'm drunk.'

We went back to the ship early as the town was full of cut-throats and thieves. I must have slept about an hour when I heard a commotion on deck. I rolled out to see what was the matter. Folley had just been brought aboard and lay unconscious on the deck. Half a dozen sailors were bending over him with a ship's lantern. His face was cut and his nose was split wide open. The blood ran everywhere. It was my first glance at the really brutal side of life. As I stood looking down at the beaten and cut body of Folley I heard some one calling in a hoarse voice for the first mate, who was the ship's doctor.

'Oh, Mr. Watson, Mr. Watson.'

CHAPTER V

THE FULL MOON AND HER VILLAINOUS CREW

WE must have been anchored in San Francisco Bay two or three months. It gave us a chance to see the city and to do a large amount of profitable trading.

The population was both gallant and lawless, generous and criminal, brave and cowardly. No one feared losing his money, for he knew that any one of a dozen friends would stake him to food, clothing, and shelter. Enormous fortunes were made and lost over the gambling tables. The knights of the western civilization were having their last fling.

I saw my Uncle Solomon every day or two. Some days we wandered along the water-front together. Often we would cross the Bay and go on horseback up into the mountains or out to my uncle's ranch, which was within an easy ride of the city. He was a man of perhaps five feet nine inches, a shade darker in color than I, yet very light for a full-blooded 'negro.' He was old and a little tired when I knew him, but he still retained something of the rugged and vigorous appearance he must have had as a younger man. As we walked or rode together he told me how he had come to San Francisco. 'I've done about everything in the world, I guess; fishing, fighting, trading, and what not, sailing my boats all over the seven seas. Just happened I was fishing off the Banks of Newfoundland in forty-nine, or was it forty-eight? Ran my little schooner into Marblehead and went ashore. Everybody chattering like a bunch of blooming monkeys. "Gold," they says, "Gold in California. Gold so thick you can pick it up by the handful." Sold my little schooner for a song, I did. Bought a barkentine like the Traveler there, and took aboard as crazy a bunch of gold-mad maniacs as you ever set eyes on. We started out for California by way of the Horn. Hit some pretty rough weather that trip. Crew was bad and the passengers were worse. Finally got out here, though. Then the crew deserted and I had to sell the boat. Nothing for me to do but buy a pick and a pan and a shovel and follow them up into the hills. I guess I've made my living, most every way you can think of. Best of all is being a skipper aboard a good, smart boat. That's what you'd better be, Sonny. It's the only life for a Dean.'

We finally left San Francisco and sailed northward to Eureka. I remember the redwood trees, forty and fifty feet in diameter. The mate, who had taken a great liking to me since my fortunate catch in the Gulf of Mexico, and who was no longer gruff or surly when I came back to fish with him off the taffrail, took me into one of the forests. 'Them trees are the oldest living things on the face of God's earth,' he told me; 'they're even older than your uncle and he ain't as young and sweet as he once was neither.'

We stopped at Astoria at the mouth of the Columbia River. It was a fishing city, the inhabitants making their living off the heavy runs of salmon which they took in nets and with hook and line. Most of the people were Indians and old friends of my uncle. One night the Indians took my uncle and me fishing for salmon. The first mate, who was next in command and therefore responsible for the ship in my uncle's absence, could not accompany us. He tried to hide his envy by declaring, he'd 'not be bothered by such small fry.' And he tried to prove that, 'Salmon ain't such a sporting fish anyhow.'

The fishing boats were large enough to hold several men. The Indians propelled the boats far out into the river and dropped anchor. We fished by the weird and wavering light of resinous torches. I caught several salmon weighing from twenty to thirty pounds. When we finally left the Indians and went aboard our ship I found myself unable to sleep. My mind was filled with the smoky flames of the torches, the sharply silhouetted faces of the Indians and the struggling of the great salmon.

At Tacoma in Puget Sound they were just commencing to build a city. Three or four hundred feet from the point in the bay where we dropped anchor they were driving in piling for a new dock. The only permanent people were the Indians. The others were a rough bunch of pioneers hard at work defacing the scenery with frame houses. The city, such as it was, amazed the Indians. But to me it was a great disappointment. Tacoma had been a name to conjure with, until I had seen it.

We were here only a day or two and one morning my uncle gave the order to up anchor. We were headed for Japan. We threaded our way out of Puget Sound and in due time reached the broad Pacific. My uncle and the first mate were always talking about making the great circle, about the weather, and about the Gulf of Alaska. I asked my uncle innumerable questions. Some of his answers left me wondering. I finally understood, however, that when he was discussing the great circle, he was discussing the nearest route between two points on the globe, and that their desire was to make Yokohama, Japan, just as soon as possible. Their hope was to avoid the adverse currents and treacherous storms that arise in the Gulf of Alaska.

We had been sailing but a few days when a wind sprang up from behind and commenced to blow strong and chill. The ship ran ahead like a frightened thing, like a hare pursued by hounds. We seemed to be racing with the waves and the clouds. Then, as if we were playing some enormous game, the wind shifted, then shifted again. It wished to encircle us and block our course with an airy, invisible wall. From each new quarter it descended upon us without mercy. We had hit rough, cold weather off Cape Horn, much colder than we were having now, but nowhere on the voyage did we encounter such high seas. It seemed as though the water, which had piled up ahead of the wind for hundreds of miles, directed all its energy into the crushing, slashing blows it dealt the ship. It was impossible to hold her to her course.

Now the talk turned to the islands, the islands, the islands. Some spoke of them with fear, and some swore softly and watched the horizon with anxious eyes. My uncle and the mate studied the charts in the cabin and shook their heads. 'What islands?' I asked. Neither of them noticed me. 'What islands?' I insisted.

The mate looked up. 'Eh, what's that? Oh, the

Aleutian Islands, Sonny, and many a good ship's gone down to Davy Jones's Locker driven against them rocky shores.'

We were running almost stripped and yet we hurtled forward like wounded quarry. Sometimes a wave hitting us squarely on the quarter would send a shudder all through the boat. Once a sailor, who with two others had gone aloft to reef a sail, lost his foothold in a sudden gust and hung dangling above the rushing sea; then with almost superhuman strength he pulled himself back to safety. . . . I began to see how small and helpless man is, and how great and how almighty the sea and the wind.

My uncle hardly took the time to eat and sleep. He never had a moment to talk to me. One evening, however, after we had eaten, he did not hurry away to the deck but sat with his head in his hands as if he were trying to think his way through some difficult problem. At last he said, 'Out here on the sea where there's nothing but a board betwixt man and death you get to thinking long, deep thoughts, Harry, thoughts you'd never think on shore. Now that fellow the other day. Was it an accident he slipped and mere luck he saved himself, or was it all mapped out like we prick a course on that chart there? I've been thinking a lot about the cause of things, and I think I've figured it out. It's fate that does it. Maybe we'll get through this storm, maybe we won't. But we can't change things much either way.' He went out on the darkening deck a few moments later, and I slipped into my oilskins and followed. I was all but swept off my feet by a gust of wind, and blinded by the salt spray. The wind was whistling and moaning through the shrouds. There was just enough light to see file on file of black seas, foaming at the crest, sweep against us. And then, under the force of a mad whirling gust of wind we were all but on our beam's end. From the companionway to the forecastle dark forms scurried. I heard their cries faint and far away. The ship staggered, hesitated, and righted herself, churning the water which had flooded the waist into a white swirling mass of foam. I heard my uncle's voice in my ear, 'This is no place for you, lad. Get back in the cabin.' As I made my way back I could hear his orders deep and clear over the uproar of the storm, and the crew's 'Aye, aye, sir,' as it scattered down the wind. That was the last I saw of the storm, relegated against my will to the comparative safety of the cabin.

By morning the wind had subsided almost as miraculously as it had arisen. The sea was still rough, but in comparison with its former fury it seemed as peaceful as an inland lake. A bleak sun shone upon us. It was the first time in days that we had seen its face. The weather continued chill but clear. Several days later we crossed the International Date Line. We were all elated that we had weathered the storm and that we were so well along on our journey.

In due time we arrived at Yokohama, Japan; and from that day until the day we left Hongkong bound for the Cocos Islands, the trip was exotic, unreal, and dreamlike. The events and impressions are interwoven in my mind like the figures and designs in tapestry. There was an Oriental pilot to guide us through these waters. I remember junks on the China Sea, yellow-skinned sailors, Hongkong and its city of boats, the trip up the river to Canton, temples on either shore, small flowering trees, petals on the dark water. Then I remember our new cargo at Canton, rice, tea, and gorgeous silks, medicinal herbs and roots, precious old jade, a set of earrings, rings and bracelets of yellow gold set with blue stones. All too soon we went back down the river.

Folley was recovering slowly and came on deck for the first time as we were about to make our departure from Hongkong for the Cocos Islands. He was convalescent and irritable. 'Sure and we're in China, ain't we? That's a fine place to be, that is. Who'd be wanting to go ashore among these heathens. They ain't human, they ain't.'

Not long after we left Hongkong we were winding in and out among channels and straits seldom out of sight of land. We went ashore on beautiful tropical islands covered with palm trees and pepper trees with bright colored birds in the foliage. On some islands the vines and verdure came right down to the water's edge, on others there were narrow sand beaches.

Sometimes when we lay at anchor we could look down through crystal water and see great sharks rolling lazily. The first mate was always harpooning them. If any one asked him why, he'd say, 'I'll fix it so a man dares wash himself hereabouts without losing a leg or an arm for his trouble.' We could have rendered a lot of oil from these sharks if we had had the facilities.

At one island where we stopped a young beach comber came aboard. He was perhaps twenty-two or three years of age. Under his ragged and torn clothes his body was strong and brown. The mate and I had just noticed a big shark not more than a dozen feet from the vessel. He was going to run for his harpoon when the beach comber stepped up.

'Gimme fifty cent. Get him with knife,' he said.

The mate gave him the coin. 'Watch him, Sonny. You'll see some fun.' I did watch with both eyes, held by a terrible fascination. The beach comber stripped, saw to his knife, and dove. Down, down he went through the crystal water with even, graceful strokes. Now he was almost under the shark, now he had drawn his arm far back for the thrust. The shark, suddenly aroused, slipped forward with a flip of his tail. We could see the boy thrust the knife upward with all his strength into the abdomen of the onrushing shark. Then the sea was clouded with blood and for a moment we saw nothing. That was a long moment. I felt sure that no man could be a match for a shark there in the great fish's own element. But the next moment the boy was climbing to the deck, smiling broadly.

'How can you do it?' I asked worshipfully.

'Easy,' he said. 'Stick knife in belly, shark swim, cut hisself open. Easy.'

Our cargo was becoming more and more valuable at every port. My uncle was very anxious to get it to Europe, so we sailed more and dropped anchor less from the Cocos Islands on. We made only one stop in India. That was Calcutta. When we made our departure from this port we sailed right across the Indian Ocean for Aden, Arabia. By the time we reached the Indian Ocean I had become quite proficient at shooting the sun and reading the vernier, but the moon with its apparent caprices was quite beyond my skill.

Here at Aden we did our business with Cowage Dinshaw, a Parsee. It was to him that we traded cargo for several of the finest Persian rugs I have ever seen, closely knotted and of rich color and design. He showered presents upon us and took us to see the wonders of Aden. He wore a skullcap and a long coat of yellow Indian silk.

The most remarkable sight at Aden was the burial of the dead. The bodies are sacrificed to the buzzards, which are considered sacred birds by all who hold to the Parsee faith. The dead body is placed upon an iron grating over a hollow tower the pit of which is filled with quicklime. As the funeral procession reaches the tower, the bones of the corpse are broken with mallets. As the ceremony ends and the mourners leave, the dark cloud of buzzards descend to their ghastly feast. As the bones are picked clean, they fall through the grating into the lime beneath.

The religion surrounding this unlovely custom is mystical and impressive and not at all unlovely. As my uncle tried to explain it to me, and as I learned in later years, the manner in which they dispose of the dead is an ingenious technique designed to save the spirit from physical transmutation. To these Parsees fire, water, and earth are the three elements. If the body were consigned to any of these, since all three are tangible and physical, the transmutation would bring the spirit of the deceased to new life in mortal form. But if the flesh is consigned to none of these, as when it is eaten by the buzzards, the spirit goes to the Parsee heaven to life immortal.

I was unable to understand the full significance of these burials and I wanted to shoot the buzzards. This shocked the good Cowage Dinshaw and would have put me in real danger had I carried out my designs on the birds. I could not understand Cowage's angry words, but my uncle told me the Parsee was saying, 'Ah, young infidel, wicked child possessed of a thousand devils, ungrateful one, is this the manner in which you repay my kindness?'

When we made our departure from Aden, we sailed across the Straits of Bab el Mandeb to a port called Berbera, then on down the coast day after day. At Zanzibar we took on ivory and spices and gums, leopard skins, hides and coffee, aromatic herbs and henna. After several weeks at Zanzibar we set sail for Lourenço Marques in the Portuguese colony. We met with unusually fine and dreamy weather in these waters. Every one was well. Folley had entirely recovered, but his face retained several ugly scars.

I had always been interested in Africa because of the stories I had been told, and because it was the continent from which my ancestors had come. Now for the first time I was sailing along its shores and my wonder and admiration grew daily. I was not satisfied with seeing its shores, however. I wanted to see its forests and jungles, its lakes and rivers. I wanted to see for myself the remnants and ruins of its glorious past. Most of my conceptions of Africa had come from my 'Arabian Chronicles.' In this glamorous old document the country had been called 'Lybia,' the heart, and had extended to the Caspian and Black Seas, including all of Arabia. Modern geographers have separated Africa from Asia at the Red Sea and the Isthmus of Suez. I preferred to think of it as I had learned it when a child.

As we sailed southward from Lourenço Marques the weather became cooler daily. Occasionally there were squalls and rain, but for the most part the weather was clear with favorable winds. Despite the bad reputation of the Cape of Storms we had little trouble in this region and dropped anchor in Table Bay at Cape Town without mishap. Here I saw for the first time the city which was to play such an important part in my later life. After perhaps a week of trading my uncle gave the command to up anchor. Soon we were bowling along toward Saldanha Bay.

So far my life had been care-free and unmotivated. I was merely living to live, in the true boyish way. I had determined in a vague way to follow the sea. No strong urge had arisen within me, however. I was floating aimlessly with the wind and the tide. But at Saldanha Bay there was an incident which brought about a sharp change in my life and started me on my quest.

The natives at Saldanha Bay were the Herreros. My uncle was a good friend of the king of this tribe and had, during his career as a sea captain, recruited several of the king's men and given them a nautical training aboard his ship. When we dropped anchor and came ashore we were given a royal welcome and for several days we stayed as the king's guests. Cattle, goats, and chickens were killed and roasted to celebrate our coming. We were offered a large hut in which to sleep and live but we declined in favor of our own comfortable cabin aboard the ship.

One evening my uncle and I were sitting on the rocks down near the beach. A full moon was riding in the sky and by its light we could see our ship where it lay at anchor in the bay. For some time we were silent, then my uncle commenced to tell me this story:

In the year 1619 a Dutch ship from the Cape named the Full Moon had come into Saldanha Bay to get water. At that time the King of the Herreros was an old man and an invalid. The Dutch captain had seen the situation and having his own unscrupulous ends in mind had devised a treacherous plan. To succeed, it had been necessary to incapacitate the King and his best men. The captain had offered his medical services to the King. He had told the King that he could make wine out of water, scare away devils, raise the dead, and a hundred other equally miraculous things; that to cure a sick man was as easy as lifting his hand. The sick old King and his counselors had been overjoyed and had allowed the Dutch captain and several of his men to come ashore. This had been exactly what the captain had wished. He had ordered the sailors to carry ashore a great quantity of Holland gin which they had proceeded to pour down the throats of the unsuspecting natives until every able-bodied man in the kraal had become dead drunk. Then when they had placed all the warriors, and the King, in a stupor, they had robbed these natives of all their valuable possessions, kidnapped sixteen little girls and four little boys all under the age of puberty and had made their departure. These defenseless children after a terrible voyage in the hold of the vessel had later been sold into slavery at Jamestown, Virginia. 'That's how it started,' my uncle concluded. 'From then on they were buying and selling men and women like so many dumb animals the length and breadth of the Colonies.'

I was incensed at the Dutch captain's wickedness. 'Why didn't they chase the Dutchmen and shoot them and bring back their little children?' I asked.

'Not a ship among them,' my uncle explained. 'That has been the downfall of our race.'

'They shall have ships, they shall have ships, they shall. . . .' I said this over and over again as I sat on the beach in the moonlight.

CHAPTER VI

IS THIS THE HILL? IS THIS THE KIRK?
IS THIS MINE OWN COUNTREE?

As we went northward toward St. Helena the sailors discussed Napoleon Bonaparte. They considered the ethical, political, and military aspects of his career. They held widely divergent opinions as to the real greatness of the man. Folley at least credited Napoleon with discretion. 'You'll notice he didn't send no army into Ireland. I suppose he says to himself, "What's the use o' sending my men to sudden death and destruction like that? It'd only take a handful of Micks to lick my whole army." . . . There's no denying he was a smart man.'

And I remember the mate's solemn words on the subject that seemed too sagacious to question and therefore closed the discussion. 'Who says, "I'm for the freedom of the seas"?' he asked. 'Napoleon. And who made 'em free? Napoleon Bonaparte. So I for one maintains he's the best friend a sailorman ever had.'

We dropped anchor at St. Helena and went ashore. We met a superior lot of colored people here. They talked English with scarcely an accent and for such an out-of-the-way part of the world were very sophisticated. The climate was better than that of California. There was no real poverty.

After several days of trading on the island my uncle gave the order to up anchor and we made our departure. We were headed for Harper, Liberia. Two things filled my mind as we sailed northward. One was the story of the Full Moon and the treacherous capture of the young natives. The other was Liberia, of which I had heard so much as a child. Slowly the two trains of thought merged into one. My desire to some day build a fleet for the Ethiopian race and thus help them to free themselves from bondage had found its immediate source in the story of the Full Moon. My knowledge that Liberia was the one bit of land in all Africa still held by its rightful heirs made me think of its importance as a base for operations. The dark continent held a new interest for me and the troubles of my race had taken on a new significance. Even at that early age I was dreaming of an Ethiopian Empire.

Our course now lay through the doldrums, a region circling the earth on either side of the Equator. Luckily we struck a period with good trade winds. At certain seasons of the year a ship may be becalmed for weeks in these latitudes, and rest motionless on glassy water under a terrific sun. We sailed for many days through a tropical sea.

Early one morning we sighted the mouth of the Cavalla River, and shortly after dropped anchor in front of Harper, Liberia. My uncle was interested in starting an observatory at Harper to observe the southern heavens, and a research laboratory to study the peculiar magnetic and electrical phenomena he had always noticed in these regions. On this particular trip, however, we merely stopped to trade and to visit some of our relatives. These relatives together with many friends overwhelmed us with kindness and generosity when we went ashore. We were feasted and fêted and given many presents.

When we had been in Harper several days, my uncle decided to make a trip up the Cavalla to visit some of our relatives who lived back in the forest. We hired a large canoe with boys to paddle it and started on the fifty-mile journey. The whole country was one great forest. There were mahogany, ebony, lignum-vitæ, rosewood, ironwood, satinwood, cedar, rubber, and hundreds of other varieties of fine trees. The woods were full of game. At night we could hear leopards and by day we often surprised a sort of pigmy hippopotamus wallowing in the mud at the edge of the river. The natives told us these were good to eat, so I determined to shoot one. I got my rifle out of the dunnage, loaded it and laid it across my knees. We paddled for several hours without sighting a hippo. Then on rounding a bend in the river we came upon a big fellow just about to enter the water. On seeing us he made a low guttural noise in his throat and plunged into the brush. The river bank at this point was fairly high and steep and it was necessary for the beast to proceed through the willow growth in a course parallel to the river. We could easily follow his clumsy movements. Finally he came to an opening in the brush where he had either to show himself or double back on his tracks. He peered out at us through suspicious little bloodshot eyes.

'Now,' my uncle whispered.

I took careful aim at his eye and pulled the trigger. He fell, and for a moment he threw himself this way and that, pawing up roots, breaking down little trees, and ripping up the moist earth. Then he lay still. We cooked several big slices of his meat. It tasted exactly like tender beef.

As we saw more and more of this country I was impressed with Africa's enormous resources. We had loaded our hold with priceless stuff all along its coast. Now, traveling inland, I saw that not a thousandth of the treasure had been looted. I realized, more than ever before, its need for ships and the fortunes awaiting those who could train and develop the Ethiopian race to appreciate their wealth and intelligently exploit it.

At last we sighted the clearing beside the river where my relatives had their cottage and small farm. We went ashore and after a short rest were ready for whatever sport the country offered. Their hunting was done in lazy-man fashion which the hot climate made very agreeable. Each night after supper a lamb was tied to a stake in the yard in front of the house, where its pitiful baa-baaing could be heard by all the beasts of prey in the vicinity. We sat in comfortable chairs on the second story porch and waited. As the evening grew darker a hyena would sneak out of the brush and make for the lamb. A shot would ring out from one of our guns and the hyena would be through lamb-stealing forever. Some evenings it would be swamp leopards instead, which made a great deal better sport. These cats were big yellow fellows with solid black spots. Beautiful hides. We took many good leopard skins during our short visit, for which we were paid well in London some months later.

They had little domesticated deer called duikers, which were fine to eat and beautiful to see. They were mild little fellows. Their color was buff with darker spots, and they had little horns. Their proportions were perfect and they would gambol over the lawn or stand and look at you out of large doe-like eyes.

When we were ready to leave, our relatives insisted on taking us up to Webbo Falls. The country about the falls is like a great garden. The falls themselves are a series of small precipitous rapids ending in a drop considerably higher than those above it. The natives had a way of testing a stranger's nerves. They would paddle as near as they dared to the falling water, and if the stranger remonstrated with them they would laugh uproariously. 'Feller get scared damn easy.' We had been warned beforehand, however, and we let the boys who were paddling our canoe take us so near that the water almost fell into the boat, narrowly escaping an upset rather than letting them have the satisfaction of seeing us frightened.

When we returned to Harper we found that the first mate had done some profitable trading in our absence. Our cargo was now a valuable one and my uncle was anxious to reach Europe. After we made our departure from Harper we dropped anchor but a few times. Sailing along the northwest coast of Africa we ran into winds coming off the Sahara Desert, winds so dry they parched our lips and dried our skin, 'Hamitan Winds' the sailors called them. We were thankful to pass through the Straits of Gibraltar and into the Mediterranean.

We stopped at Quata in Morocco, where we saw some of my father's people. All along the coast here at Tunis and at Tripoli the water was crowded with small Arabian craft with graceful lateen sails of rainbow colors. They looked more like a flight of sea-birds than like ships. We dropped anchor at Alexandria and took several trips inland. We went up the Nile as far as Cairo. This was my first experience with the historic river. Later I was to travel its whole length and to sit at dawn at the outlet of Lake Nyanza where the river springs, watching the clear water flow over the rock of Jinja in a miniature waterfall as it starts its long journey toward the Mediterranean. I was to see in later years unbelievable treasures along its banks of which the world is still unaware.

We stopped at several ports, each one more romantic than the last. At Genoa we visited the home of Columbus. Here we attended an opera that lasted three days and three nights. There were three hundred pieces in the orchestra and fifteen hundred voices in the chorus. There was hardly a bass voice among them. I remember the leader of the orchestra had long black hair. He grew so emotional over one passage in the music, and swung himself about so vigorously, that he fell over backward. He never ceased waving the baton, however, and while he was on the floor, and during the moments he was rising to his feet, he continued to lead the orchestra through a difficult part of the music.

I have a particularly good reason for remembering Naples. We were anchored in the bay for several days. Each evening we would go ashore to eat at one of the many little restaurants where one sits at tables on the sidewalk and eats spaghetti and sardines and drinks wine. On the evening before our departure we came as usual to order our meal and to sit and watch these temperamental people and hear their rapid musical language. On this particular evening, however, something was wrong. The little groups at the tables were talking in hushed but excited tones. Our waiter was so preoccupied that my uncle had to repeat the order twice. People glanced nervously up the narrow cobblestoned street toward a corner half a block distant where several streets converged. Suddenly, almost without warning, a mob poured around the corner from one of the side streets, surrounded an unpretentious stone building some two hundred yards from where we were sitting, and commenced breaking in the doors and shattering the windows. Several shots were fired from within. Several of the men at the tables, leaping to their feet, reached for their weapons. The waiter dropped the wine and spaghetti he was about to serve us and drawing a wicked-looking stiletto from under his belt dived headlong into the affray. Men gathered from everywhere to fight the assailants. Before we had a chance to move, the mob fight was under way and had spread almost to where we were sitting. We were lucky to escape with our lives. My uncle fairly picked me off my feet as he dragged me out of danger. We could hear the high-pitched screams, and when we turned to look five or six bodies lay bleeding on the cobblestones. By this time the soldiers had been aroused. They rushed past us down the narrow street while the mob dispersed in all directions. That night in my own safe bunk in the cabin I dreamed fantastic nightmares of stilettos and soldiers and black-mustached Italians.

At Marseilles my uncle and I left the ship to do the Continent. It was April when we went ashore. All through the spring and summer and early fall we traveled in France, Germany, Poland, and Russia. My uncle had made a good profit from the rugs and ivory and spices he had sold at Marseilles and our trip was in the way of a celebration. At some of the towns where we stopped he did business for the ship, but in general we merely traveled, stopped at good hotels, enjoyed the plays we saw, the music we heard, and the fine weather. Meanwhile Mr. Watson, the first mate, had sailed the ship around to Southampton. At the first sign of frost we went to England and aboard the Traveler. We sailed her up to London and there the major trading of the trip occurred.

The principles of trading as I learned them then, and to a greater degree later in life, depend entirely upon supply and demand. One must know the best market for each part of his cargo. In some parts of Africa a bolt of red cloth is worth a lot of ivory. The cloth is of use to the natives, the ivory is not. In England the cloth is worth a few cents a yard and the ivory thousands of dollars. The ship had left New York laden with a cargo of fairly inexpensive staples. By intelligent trading our cargo became more and more valuable from port to port. By the time we arrived at London we were loaded with spices, rare skins, herbs and dyes, ivory, jewelry, priceless jade, ostrich feathers, and mohair as well as less valuable cargo. We sold most of our jade and jewelry in London as Americans in those days had no appreciation for antique Chinese ornaments. We took on a fine grade of English cloths, cashmere shawls, and prepared seal-skins, and received a liberal balance in cash. The trading operations went on all winter and we had time to visit many parts of the British Isles.

When spring came we made a record trip to Boston, encountering little bad weather with the exception of fog off Newfoundland. When we dropped anchor at Boston, cherry trees were in bloom. And there I left the crew of Traveler the Second. With the exception of my uncle I was never to see them again. I said good-bye to the first mate, the bos'n, Folley, Old John-son the steward, and to ever so many more of the men who had become my friends during our three years together. They all gave me presents to remember them by. The first mate kept blowing his nose and muttering something about 'The dod-blasted wind makin' his eyes water.' Soon I was aboard a train bound for home. Thus after a three-year voyage I returned to my parents in Philadelphia, having cir-cumnavigated the globe by the age of fifteen.

BOOK II
THE PEDRO GORINO

CHAPTER VII

STAVANGER AND THE PEDRO GORINO

I SPENT the rest of my youth in securing an education in the arts and sciences of the sea. My quest for knowledge and adventure took me to the ends of the world. It was a strenuous, tragic, and terrible part of my life; often I was at the mercy of heartless men.[1] But through travail and toil I still retained in the back of my mind the story of the Full Moon and her sorry cargo. And I determined some day to start a campaign based upon the eternal truth that a race without ships is like a man stricken and blind. I would instigate a movement to rehabilitate Africa and found such an Ethiopian Empire as the world has never seen. It would be greater than the empire in Haiti, for while that island kingdom with its Toussaint l'Ouvertures and Christophes produced great palaces, and forts, and armies — battalions strong enough to whip the best soldiery of France — yet the island itself is a mere pin-point on the earth's surface compared to the great continent of Africa where I planned to build my empire. It would be greater than the empires of Africa's past — such powerful nations as those who raised their enormous stone structures at Zimbabwe and elsewhere — for although these kingdoms must have numbered their subjects by the hundreds of thousands, their store of knowledge was limited. I

[1] I hope some day he will publish his adventures during these years. So far he refuses even to talk of them. Something very terrible or tragic keeps him silent. (S. North.)

dreamed of an empire infinitely more cultured. Africa could again lift up her head. Her fleets would sail upon the sea. Her resources would once more enrich her own children. I dreamed of downfall for the imperialists, those wolves from the Zuider Zee and the slums of White Chapel.

Fortunately for my project I met Captain Forbes early in life. He became my patron and sponsor just as Clarkson and Wilberforce had been Paul Cuffee's. To him I attribute what I possess of the higher reaches of nautical science. He it was who taught me the theory and technique of international maritime practice.

Captain Forbes looked something like Sir John Fisher. He was slender and dark skinned with a Norman profile. He was quick and accurate in conversation, devastating in debate. We became great friends as our views were all in harmony. He was a humanitarian and a universalist with the good of the whole world at heart. I was no less a humanitarian, but my particular object was the betterment of the Ethiopian race.

Before I could even begin to help my people it was necessary to secure a ship. One day Captain Forbes came to me with the news that Count Thesen of Norway, one of his very good friends, had just such a ship as I had been seeking. It lay at anchor at Stavanger, Norway, and it was necessary for us to journey there if we wished to make arrangements for its purchase. We took passage on a steamer bound for Norway.

There were three of us who went up to Stavanger,

Captain Forbes, Sydney Wilson, and I. I had found
Sydney Wilson sitting on a park bench in Leicester
Square, London. He was a rawboned Basian, shiny
black and as strong as a bull. I could tell by the cut
of his jib that he was as true as steel. He had run away
from his ship after having been badly treated. He told
me about his troubles in his deep, musical, West Indian
brogue. 'Been sailin' since I was pickaninny. Seen
some billows. Never seen mate like de mate on dat
ship. Dat buck of a man tink I'm a fool. He whip me.
I knock him down and run away from ship.' I determined then and there to take him with me if I
found a boat. Before many weeks had passed I was to
find that he was a fearless sailor and an excellent cook.

As we three traveled northward aboard the steamer
we watched the northern lights which until this time
I had never seen in such brilliance. As we approached
the coast of Norway we sat transfixed at the magnificent scenery. Neither Sydney Wilson nor I in all our
travels had seen these fjords and cliffs and snow-capped
mountains. The water was blue and clear. The land
seemed clean and unlittered. On the hilly meadows
cattle grazed. Here and there dark forests came down
to the sea. But more miraculous than all else were the
mountains that were not mountains at all, phantom
hills and cliffs through which the eye could penetrate
to valleys and green pastures beyond.

Before we realized it our journey was over and we
were at Stavanger, Norway. We found the little city
quite as clean as the hilly meadows along the coast.
The fishermen's cottages with their quaint gardens
were bright and colorful. I was impressed with the

gentility, refinement, and quiet culture of these people. They seemed positive but just, deliberate but intelligent; people who could understand the realities of life yet with men among them who could dream as well as any.

The day after our arrival we went to the offices of Thesen and Company. The count himself was in South Africa, but his agent made us welcome and told us about the boat. We all went down to the dock together. The water was crowded with fishing boats and small craft of every kind. One among them seemed as proud as a swan in a flock of wild geese. She was the ship we hoped to buy. I have sailed aboard many boats in my life, but not one was as graceful as this. She was a freak topsail schooner rigged to carry a great mass of canvas. She was some seventy feet long with the lines of a greyhound. She had what is known as a 'pink' stern, a stern almost as high and pointed as the prow, giving the boat an unusual symmetry. And although her two masts were bare I could picture them with white canvas bellying in the wind.

We took a skiff and went aboard. We examined her from stem to stern. She was the worthy product of the sons of the Vikings and as strong as the day she was launched. Her strakes and wales were of oak, staunch enough for a man-of-war. When I went into the hold I found the keelson of enormous strength as were the garboard strakes. The way things were shored and braced would have delighted any sailor. Every point in the whole boat where there was any stress was made of oak. She had been given such good

care she was really better than new. She was a sea-
soned boat. We found no defects in the stays or
shrouds, clamps or yards. And although we searched
for rot with our pocket knives we could find none.
Above all she was beautifully and newly copper-
sheathed. I realized from our examination that she
would hold herself to a course and carry sail without
lying on her side.

The name on the prow was almost obliterated by the
weather so we hunted up her log. The name was the
'Pellar Guri,' and beneath the name was a page of
illuminated script which Captain Forbes translated.
It ran something like this:

In the early part of the fifteenth century, Norway was
under the sway of independent robber barons. There was
one tyrant who became so cruel and greedy that the people
drove him from the land. He escaped to Scotland where he
bribed a Scottish chief named Sinclair to assist him in con-
quering Norway. Together these schemers gathered a huge
army and descended upon the unsuspecting Norwegians.
There was a peasant girl named Pellar Guri living in one
of the valleys. With great courage and spirit she rallied all
the peasants of Norway and drove the robber and his hirelings from the land. From this united effort rose the Kingdom
of Norway.

The boat had been named for this heroic girl, and
the figurehead was a fine representation of her strength
and beauty. Sydney Wilson, who was a West Indian
and who had been under Spanish influence all his life,
misunderstood the name, however. He thought we
had said the Pedro Gorino. He was a clever man with
the brush as most sailors are, and several days later he

took it upon himself to paint the name on the prow. He led me proudly to the dock to show me his handiwork.

'But that isn't her name,' I protested, 'her name is the Pellar Guri.'

'Pellar Guri no name for black man's ship,' he replied. And he looked so dejected when I suggested changing it that I said no more about it. And Pedro Gorino she was from that day forth.

I attribute to Captain Forbes all my success in this deal for the Pedro Gorino. He arranged such liberal terms with Thesen's agent that I took a new lease on life. Before the week was out he had solved another of our problems. The ship was without sails and he had found an extraordinary bargain. We went up to see the sail-makers in their loft. There were a dozen old salts sewing away on canvas for all they were worth. The light fell upon them from little windows opening out over the sea. Ah, there was a scene for a great master, the light falling upon those old men and the character in their faces.

Captain Forbes could talk Norwegian and most of the men could talk good English so we understood each other very nicely. When they heard my story and found that I was going out to South Africa they informed us of an extraordinary coincidence. They had in another loft connected with their organization sixteen young men who for several months had been preparing to go to South Africa to seek their fortune. They were all young sailors and it came to my mind that they might be willing to man the ship and sail her out to Cape Town for their passage. We met the young sailmakers later that afternoon and they were eager to accept our terms. Consequently we drew up a contract with these people purchasing the gear and sails and arranging for the exchange of the services of these young men for their passage to South Africa.

The next day we opened ship and commenced to take in stores. There was practically no repair work necessary, but we gave the boat a thorough inspection and overhauling. Within the scheduled time the sails were aboard and the crew was ready for the journey. They were as fine and clean cut a bunch of boys as I have known. There were fifteen Norwegians, one Scotchman, Sydney Wilson cook par excellence, Captain Forbes, and I. One of the Norwegians, Captain Carlson, was a very experienced mariner so I made him my first mate. We took aboard the last of our hundred tons of cargo and luggage and prepared to up anchor.

The next morning we made our departure and plotted a great circle for England. The North Sea was choppy and we hit rather rough weather during the first part of our trip. It was cold and rainy with leaden-colored skies overhead. The Pedro Gorino responded to our every touch, and proved herself a fine, seaworthy little ship. In several days we sighted the lights eighty miles northeast of London and were soon in the channel. We shaped our course due west by south with a favorable breeze and finally dropped anchor at Southampton.

I was very sorry to have to leave Captain Forbes, but our parting at Southampton was inevitable as his business held him in England. While we were at anchor he gave me literally tons of useful cargo and dozens of nautical instruments. Among his gifts were sextants, books, charts and maps, three fine solar chronometers, two sidereal chronometers, a four-inch telescope, and a muzzle-loading salute cannon. The cannon proved to be not the least serviceable of these, and on one occasion saved us from a real catastrophe. The captain went with us as far as the Lizards, the point where ships leaving England make their departure. We had a sorrowful parting and he promised to come to South Africa within the year. When he could accompany us no farther he hailed a pilot boat and stepped aboard, leaving me to the great task we had planned together.

We plotted our course in a great circle from the Lizards to Funchal, and went bowling along piling up knot after knot. Far out on the wild Atlantic we had no thought of the Biscayan tides, but were surrounded by porpoises even before we came to cloudless Madeira and the pearl Teneriffe set as they were in a sea of glass.

The Scotchman aboard our ship was a great story-teller as were one or two of the Norwegians. The weather was fine and there was little work and much time for games and stories. I remember one story the Scotchman told the name of which was, *All About Jonah and His Voyage in the Belly of the Whale.* It is a raw story and one to which religious people might take exception, so for the sake of discretion *I* had better not relate it.

The Scotchman, however, had no such scruples. He would say, 'Hoot mon, that's nae story. Listen to this one.' Whereupon we would receive another deluge of his racy narration. He knew most of Bobby Burns by heart; and his favorite poem was,

> ' Ye flowery banks o' bonnie Doon,
> How can ye blume sae fair?
> How can ye chant, ye little birds,
> And I sae fu' o' care? '

Finally we made landfall at Madeira and dropped anchor at Funchal. Here we took on water and provisions and I invested the rest of my money in Madeira lace and carved furniture of rare woods which I knew I could sell at a profit at Cape Town. Soon we made our departure, and putting up every bit of rag we could carry, sailed day after day ahead of a light but favorable breeze. We passed the peaks of Teneriffe off the coast of Rio de Oro and after uneventful sailing sighted St. Vincent in the Cape Verde Islands.

So far we had encountered good weather, but one morning the sun arose red-yellow and we knew we were in for a storm. We shaped our course due south under full sail trying to miss its path and sail out of danger, but by noon the wind had slackened until the ship scarcely moved through the water. By mid-afternoon there was not a breath of air save for an occasional puff from every quarter which only served to make the sails flap idly where they hung. A haze began to spread over the ocean. This and the peculiar color of the sky told us more plainly than words what to expect. We put things in shipshape and waited. We must have lain becalmed over an hour laboring for breath in the hot sultry air, the ship rolling quietly on the glassy water. Suddenly we noticed a disturbance in the haze several hundred yards off our starboard. Then out of the ocean arose a great water-spout drawn higher and higher by a powerful wind which whirled like a corkscrew. The great column of water a hundred feet high was headed for the ship and came down upon us at an enormous rate of speed. But the wind that brought it did not fill our sails and we lay helpless, directly in the path of the oncoming disaster. I had once been aboard a ship when a small waterspout passed near throwing tons of water over the midship and taking several men from their feet. I remembered how the ship had staggered under the impact, and in the second I had for thought I realized that this great column of water rushing down upon us might easily send us to the bottom. Then in the nick of time I remembered the advice of my old Uncle Silas. 'If a spout comes at you shoot it with a gun. It'll fall same as any living thing.' Our salute cannon mounted on the bow was always filled with shot and powder. I rushed to this and, aiming it at the oncoming pillar of water, fired. The waterspout broke at less than fifty yards from the ship and poured back into the sea like a waterfall. We were very thankful for our deliverance. Within a few hours a breeze sprang up from the port quarter and we got a splendid run all the evening.

We sighted St. Paul on our port some days later and continued to sail day after day through an untroubled sea. We plotted our course southeast and piled up knot after knot of southern latitude. As we approached St. Helena the weather grew squally but we would not shorten sail. We passed outside the island, only sighting her hills. The menacing sky kept us on the alert, but the splendid stiffness of our lady Pedro Gorino held to her course and would not give an inch, but instead gained to windward and mounted the waves like a Guinea goose.

At last we sighted Table Mountain and the Lion's Rump without mishap or accident, having made our reckoning to the second of a degree. Thus we came to Cape Town from Stavanger, Norway, in seventy-one days on the good ship the Pedro Gorino.

CHAPTER VIII

CAPE TOWN, A SOMALI PRINCE, AND A TEXAS COWBOY

WHEN we dropped anchor in Table Bay we found the harbor crowded with warships and transports. South Africa was in the throes of the Boer War. We might have been in quarantine for many days, but the agent of Thesen and Company arranged to secure us pratique and we were soon ashore. As I stood on the dock looking back across the bay the Pedro Gorino seemed very small and helpless among the great men-of-war.

I had no trouble in selling my cargo at a profit and paying Count Thesen the balance I owed on the Pedro Gorino. The Count was Consul-General for the Kingdom of Norway, but I found him to be a very democratic and unassuming nobleman. Shortly after my arrival he invited me out to his beautiful estate. I have forgotten the name of the place, but it was Norwegian and was designed to embrace the concept of a view of the sea, the mountains, and the forest. After an enjoyable week-end we returned to Cape Town together. All along the peninsula we passed estate after estate of English gentlemen, among others the estate of Cecil Rhodes.

But not all the inhabitants of Cape Town were of the caliber of the Norwegian Consul. Ever since the old Dutchman, Van Riebeek, and his motley crew of Hollanders stole South Africa from the Hottentots there has been race admixture. This was true to such an extent that when I was in South Africa classification was by rule rather than by nature. Much to my surprise, and despite my protests the authorities insisted upon classifying me as European because of my European training and my light color. Strange to say, the authorities and the inhabitants disagreed, which put me in the wrong light with all factions. I was suspected of social climbing when I mixed with the European Colonials and suspected by the government of ulterior motives when I mixed with my own race.

I realized the danger of my position, but I had decided to make Cape Town my headquarters and I was not to be easily dissuaded. I realized that the Cape was the most strategic point in that part of the world and was bound to become as important as the Golden Horn in ancient times. I realized also that while I was awaiting my chance to help the Ethiopian race I could not do better than locate in the very midst of the imperialists and learn their game at first hand. I had some difficulty in finding an office for my shipping business, but finally through the assistance of Freighter and Elliott I was able to locate on the Strand.

There was a coffee house on Hanover Street, a typical English coffee house, two steps up with little green tables and a silver urn for making cocoa. It was run by an Africando, a congenial old fellow. It was here that I picked up some of my best friends, men who were to play an important part in the next few years of my life. Here it was that I picked up a new crew to replace the Norwegians who sailed the ship to Cape Town. Among the first were Peter Benjamin and Will Braithwaith from Barbados. They were both intelligent fellows and just the sort I was looking for.

One evening some two weeks after my arrival I went as usual to the coffee house for my evening meal. At one of the tables sat three strangers, one of whom was colored. By their accent I knew that they were Americans. I was so elated to see Americans again that I said in a rather gruff voice, 'What are you boys doing around here?'

The colored fellow seemed to sense hostility in my voice. 'We ain't asking nobody no questions,' he answered, glowering darkly.

'I'm an American myself,' I explained. 'And it's seldom enough one meets a man from home in this part of the world.'

'Well, if you wasn't meanin' to insult us, let's shake on it,' the big 'negro' suggested.

It was perhaps well that I had ignored the challenge in the first words he had spoken, for I was to find that Kid Gardener, the colored fellow, was a two-fisted buck from Texas with a six-shooter and a long knife. That this cowboy was also a good sort was not so obvious. These men had come to Cape Town on a ship from New Orleans carrying stores from the States for the British Government. Being rovers they wanted to see more of the war, but they were out of money, out of whiskey, and out of sorts with the world in general.

I offered them the hospitality of my ship until I started trading again, and tried to dissuade them from trying to get through to Kimberley. Kid Gardener accepted my offer but the other two were tired of Cape Town and declined with thanks. The Kid and I became great friends, and I found that although he was a desperado he was chivalrous at heart.

One warm evening as we sat outside the coffee house looking up at the bright heavens and talking of the thousand and one things sailors and adventurers talk about, we saw a little group of Cape Malays across the street talking earnestly. An old frequenter of the place pointed out one of them and said, 'That's Haji Hassan, the richest Mohammedan in South Africa.' I was interested and asked about the man. I found that Hassan was a mysterious figure. No one knew how he made his wealth or what he had done to be so powerful among the Mohammedans of South Africa, but every one knew that he was powerful. Rumors varied; some said he was a Somali prince, some said he was a quiet Arabian scholar and a very religious man, having made frequent pilgrimages to Mecca as his given name would indicate. But every one agreed that there was something uncanny about the man. He was said to know every important turn in the war even before the papers. He had inside information on all the unsolved crimes. My informer pointed to a short wiry man by Haji's side. 'That is Hamid Abdurraman, one of Haji's right-hand men,' he said.

Later in the evening the Kid and I had a chance to meet Haji and Hamid. They strolled nonchalantly across the street and acknowledged the introduction with a slight bow. Although they had been quite out of hearing all the evening I had a strangely apprehensive feeling that they had heard every word of our conversation. Hamid would not have attracted a second glance but Haji was one of the most striking men I have ever seen. He was a princely looking black-skinned fellow, tall and strong with a handsome, intelligent face. His lips were thin and well formed, his nose slightly aquiline. His most striking feature, however, was neither the thin lips nor the long slender nose but his eyes, which seemed to glow like the eyes of a great cat. Once or twice before I had seen such eyes, the iris encircled with a yellow ring, the pupil dark and piercing. I knew that I was dealing with no ordinary man.

I was interested; the Kid was hypnotized. In the days that followed Haji and I became friends, but Haji and the Kid were soon thicker than thieves in a mysterious business, the nature of which remained unknown to me for some months.

Several days later Haji Hassan left town for Kimberley on a protracted visit. Before leaving, however, he made Hamid Abdurraman vouch for Kid Gardener's discretion and conduct in the interim. Haji realized that the Kid had the type of temper that might lead him amuck at any time, and because the Texan was such a valuable man Haji was taking no chances. Further to secure matters, he asked me to help Hamid if anything went wrong.

The Kid no longer needed my hospitality, but he still needed my friendship. The day after Haji's departure he came aboard the Pedro Gorino to make me a visit. The ship at this time was employed in hauling fishing boats up and down the peninsula. As we sailed eastward the Kid and I talked together. He seemed to have fallen into miraculously good fortune, for as he sat beside me on the deck he smoked an expensive cigar and waved bediamonded hands.

I asked him to tell me about Haji Hassan.

'He's a straight-shootin' sort,' the Kid confided. 'He's the sort I like to get connected up with.' Then he told me almost all he knew about Haji, but I knew there was something he was keeping from me. It seems that Haji had been a prince among the Somalis but, discontented with his rôle, had decided to see more of the world. After going to Mecca and making his hadj he became interested in the city of Aden, where he had gone into business with Cowage Dinshaw, whom I had met as a boy. Often he would travel up and down the coast of Africa and of Arabia as Cowage's special agent. On one of these trips he learned of a diamond rush in South Africa. Like hundreds of others he hurried to the region about Kimberley. He never returned to Aden nor to his people the Somalis.

As the Kid sat beside me telling Haji's story it seemed quite natural that the absolutely fearless, handsome, mysterious Somali should have taken a fancy to the recklessly daring, brilliantly foolhardy, Texas cowboy. I was piqued to know their game, however. This the Texan refused to reveal, becoming suddenly cold and quiet at my question.

Early one morning several days later as I was standing upon the dock I saw Hamid Abdurraman hurry toward me. He seemed troubled. 'What's the matter, Hamid?' I asked.

He was so breathless that all he could say was, 'Allah have mercy.' Finally he recovered enough to tell his story: He and Kid Gardener had been walking up Caledon Street on the previous evening and having passed through the Mohammedan district had proceeded into the European section of town. As they were passing a pub the Kid had suggested that they go in and have a drink. Hamid, knowing that there would be trouble if a colored man entered a European saloon, tried to dissuade him. The Texan, however, was not to be dissuaded. He swaggered in through the half doors and up to the bar. Hamid, knowing the unwritten law of Cape Town, and being a Mohammedan and an abstainer, remained at the latticed door of the saloon prepared to give what aid he could if worst came to worst.

The Kid ordered ale and was served by the barmaid. Hamid drew a long breath and waited. There were a number of Englishmen and Boers in the barroom, but the Texan drank his glass as leisurely as if there were no one in sight. Then he ordered a pint bottle of whisky. The proprietor who had just noticed him said to the barmaid, 'Hold on there, girl.'

'What's the meanin' of this? You tryin' to insult me?' the Kid asked.

'Get out, swartz,' the proprietor shouted.

The Kid's voice was like steel. 'You trying to class me with your Cape Town nigguhs? I'm from Texas, and I ain't to be tampered with.'

The proprietor grabbed for a bottle, and the Kid prepared to jump over the bar and finish the argument in the only convincing way he knew. At that moment, however, a new element entered into the fight. Two British secret service men who had been sitting at a near-by table jumped to their feet and threw themselves upon the Texan. The proprietor, fearing he would hit one of the Englishmen, did not throw the upraised bottle.

The Kid threw them off, and with a sharp left hook sent his first assailant reeling to the floor. The second drew a gun which the Texan deftly kicked from his hand, disabling several of the Englishman's fingers. At this moment the proprietor threw his bottle. The Kid ducked but it nicked him on the side of the head before it crashed against the opposite wall. By this time the first man was on his feet again. He raised a chair high above his head and brought it down with all his strength upon the Texan. It was a blow that would have killed the ordinary man, but Kid Gardener, superb fighter that he was, sank slowly to his knees, still retaining enough consciousness to draw from under his belt a long, wicked-looking knife. As the two Britishers jumped on the fallen cowboy he lashed out left and right, cutting the man who had knocked him down from the ear to the tip of his chin, almost taking his jugular vein. At this point, some two or three minutes after the Kid had entered the barroom, little Hamid Abdurraman rushed in and tried to defend his charge, but the excited crowd who had double-banked and almost killed the Kid took no notice of the small figure of Hamid. A moment later officers of the law poured in from the street to quell the tumult. They took the Kid to jail, half dragging, half carrying his cut and bruised body.

Hamid had searched for me all over town, but despite his frantic efforts it was not until the following morning that he had found me to tell me the story. I decided that there was but one chance for the Kid. We must establish the fact that he was American by birth and secure the aid of the American Consul. I hurried immediately to the consul's office.

He was an anæmic old man from Kansas; I have forgotten his name. He said that he had been a railway conductor but he looked more like a retired farmer to me. He was so illiterate that it was only with the greatest difficulty that he could spell out a letter of introduction to the Chief of Police. The letter safely in my pocket I hurried to police headquarters to request a pass for the consul and for me, so that we might see Kid Gardener where he lay in jail. The Chief of Police, who was a great fat Boer with a fair command of English, read and reread the letter until I thought he must be trying to memorize it. Finally he looked at me over his glasses and grunted, 'You want a pass?'

I said, 'The letter speaks for itself.'

'Give the consul one, not you.'

'Suit yourself,' I replied, trying to seem calm. He called his clerk and made out a pass. I immediately carried it to the consul. He stared at it rather blankly and said,

'Oh, yes, yes, the pass. I'll see him one of these days.'

'Don't bother,' I said, at last losing my temper. . . .

Whether or not the Kid was in the right — and I have always held that he was since he was fighting in self-defense against uneven odds — I was determined to do everything within my power to help him. I wished desperately that Haji Hassan had been there, but since he was not, and since the American Consul was quite useless, I prepared to handle matters as best I could. First I went to a big store in Cape Town and instructed one of the clerks to get Kid Gardener's order, fill it, and send me the bill. Satisfied that he would have good clothes and food until the day of his trial, I went and saw my barrister and solicitor, men I had retained for my sea business. They agreed to take the case and there was nothing to do but await the unhappy day.

The prison camp at Cape Town is called 'The Breakwater.' I could not bear to think of the Kid serving a term within its cruel walls. I have seen prison systems the world over but nothing worse than the one in South Africa. Through their effective court system, British politicians impress great hordes of men, both guilty and innocent, into back-breaking work on the breakwater and in the quarries. They doubtless gild their own pockets with the money saved on construction costs. Great numbers arrive from the region around Kimberley to serve long sentences for having been caught with uncut diamonds in their possession. For, no matter how honestly a native comes by one of these stones, even if he were to find it in his own kraal, he is certain, if discovered, to serve a term on the breakwater, occasionally a life sentence. The natives are quite unable to defend themselves in the courts, and almost every one accused of a crime is convicted. These poor fellows are dressed in white duck to create an illusion of humanitarianism among outsiders. To one who knows the real conditions the dress is sinister. When I was in Cape Town this subtle form of slavery still existed long after outright slavery had been abolished throughout the civilized world.

Was it any wonder that I wished to save my friend? To have his free spirit and adventurous nature cooped within prison walls was like clipping the wings of a brilliant cock, or harnessing a stallion to the plow. . . .

Finally the case came to court. The Kid was given four years. I could do nothing but accept his fate.

CHAPTER IX

A TRAMP SHIP ON THE INDIAN OCEAN

It was not long before I had gathered together a good crew. Sydney Wilson, my cook and steward, came out with me from England. He stayed with the Pedro Gorino from first to last. Captain Peter Benjamin, my first mate, was from Barbados. He was the last colored man to graduate from the Liverpool Nautical College and a very competent and dependable mariner. In many ways he reminded me of the bos'n on Traveler the Second, for he had no neck at all, was short and heavy set, and was as black a man as the world has ever seen. He was every bit as kindly and as generous as the bos'n had been, but he was a great deal more intelligent.

Will Braithwaith, my second mate, was also from Barbados. His grandfather had been a recognized poet on that island and he had a touch of the poet in his nature. One of the family traditions told of English nobility in his ancestry; however that may be, his color was light and his features slightly Caucasian. He had had an English university education and spoke as gently as a woman and as perfectly as the Prince of Wales. His nature was the most complex and paradoxical I have ever known. Despite his apparently gentle ways he was the toughest sailor and the greatest fighter I have ever met. He did not drink, but he was always broke. He seemed to like his work aboard ship but he was the first man to go ashore when we reached port.

On shore he wore a Prince Albert coat, a tall silk hat, and neatly creased trousers. He always carried a cane. He wrought absolute havoc with the ladies.

The rest of the crew, with the exception of four native Africans, were from South America and the West Indies. They were a good crew, and they took a particular interest in the operations of the ship because of a profit-sharing plan I instituted aboard the Pedro Gorino.

Through the aid of Freighter and Elliott, Thesen and Company, and several influential friends on the dock I was able to arrange for a regular freight and passenger business. Much of the work on the dock and in Cape Town was done by natives who came from their home kraals under contract to labor for three to six months at a shilling a day. Contracts were continually expiring and new contracts being made, so there was a considerable flux of native labor up and down the coast. I made contracts to transport these men. We improvised a service for passengers by building a superstructure on the deck. Their quarters were very comfortable. On our first trip we carried forty passengers bound for Port Elizabeth, East London, and Port St. John's, together with their luggage and a full miscellaneous cargo.

Because of our Norwegian registry and because of the extreme importance of maintaining our neutrality in those troubled times we flew the Norwegian flag. We made our departure from Table Bay under a cloud of sail. I doubt if a more enthusiastic or adventurous crew ever manned a Scandinavian ship. We were dark brown Vikings on an African coast ready for wind and rough weather, yet to the prosaic men with whom we did our business we were nothing but a tramp ship on the Indian Ocean.

The native passengers whom we had taken aboard had lived all their lives on a diet of milk and mealies as if they had been children. Only occasionally had they eaten meat in their own kraals or at Cape Town. I had arranged to give them a regular board-of-trade fare. Sydney Wilson was an excellent cook and his four meals a day were delicious. The natives, who were an unsophisticated lot, tried to gorge themselves at every meal.

When they got over their seasickness many of them showed signs of making good mariners. They learned a great deal about sailing in the short time they were aboard. It set me wondering why the British government did not encourage these people to lead a maritime life. Instead it seemed that they did everything possible to keep them from the sea.

We rounded Cape Agulhas, which is the southernmost point of Africa, and proceeded eastward along a rocky coast. Driven by favorable winds we passed outside Mossel Bay and Knysna, and at last dropped anchor at Port Elizabeth.

This little city nestles in a great natural amphitheater overlooking the harbor. We found it very congenial. There were several fine churches and a great municipal market here. To this market the Boer farmers drive their enormous wagons drawn by sixteen oxen. With great shouting, creaking of wheels, and cracking of whips these wagons lumber into town. At the market government officials sell the produce for every shilling it will bring, charging the farmer but a small fee for their service. It was through this channel that the agents of Freighter and Elliott had accumulated the cargo we now took aboard. There were leopard, cheetah, and buckskins, the hides of cattle and goats, and above all mohair and buchu leaves. We put ashore a cargo of hardware and drygoods, as well as several passengers bound for this port.

Our trip from Port Elizabeth to East London was thoroughly pleasant as the weather was warm and the wind favorable. We reached our destination and dropped anchor in the open roadstead early one morning. I remember that the beach was lined with great boulders and unless a vessel had perfect ground tackle it was in constant danger from southeasters. The lack of protection here made it doubly necessary for a ship to be well anchored, for if she were not, the wind might send her ashore to break on the rocks. There was a hulk within a few hundred yards of where we were anchored and I became curious about it.

Braithwaith knew the story of the wreck and told it to me. The ship had been an American barque and she had come to East London with a valuable miscellaneous cargo of some three thousand tons. She had completed her trading operations and was preparing to up anchor when a southeaster hit her. For a short time she held her ground, but as the wind grew stronger and the whitecaps lashed about her, and the waves came rolling over her, she began to drag anchor. All the people of the city had come down to the beach, but not one could think of any way in which they could render aid to the distressed ship. All that they could do was to stand along the semicircular beach like the audience at a play watching the tragedy enacted to its bitter end. The crew seemed perfectly helpless as they stood there on the deck watching the ship come nearer and nearer to the rocks. But when it had been driven within a hundred yards of the shore and it was only a matter of minutes until the final crash, the people had seen a small sturdy sailor throw off his shoes and shirt, tie a rope around his waist, mount the rail, and plunge into the raging surf. When his head came above after the dive the whole populace cheered. To swim in such a sea is next to impossible, but in some manner he had made the shore, bringing with him the life rope over which every member of the crew made his way to safety. The people had carried on their shoulders the sailors to their homes, where they gave them hot drinks and dry clothing. The ship and cargo had been lost, however, and the hulk lying in the roadstead was all that was left to commemorate the event.

At East London I met Kirkland Soga, editor of one of the very few newspapers ever printed in a native African tongue. His mother was a Scotch missionary and his father chief of a Kosar tribe. His father had translated both the Bible and Pilgrim's Progress into Kosar, and was the first native of South Africa to attract the interest of a biographer.

The old chief's name was Teo Soga, more Japanese than African. Kirkland Soga attempted to explain it through an old tradition he had heard. The story runs that before the cataclysm South Africa, Madagascar, Sumatra, Java, and even Korea and Japan were all connected by land and formed a great, illustrious, and powerful empire. The people were highly cultured, the rulers rich and wise. When the great flood came over the land it left only the remote provinces. However that may be, one may still find such Japanese names as Teo Soga on the coast of Africa to this very day.

Because of our dangerous position in the roadstead, we were glad to up anchor and make our departure for Port St. John's at the mouth of the St. John's River, which stream divides Pondo Land from the Transkei. As we sailed along the coast I became entranced with the sight of high green hills rising obliquely out of the sea, covered with dense subtropical vegetation. The joy of the natives at seeing their own country again was quite moving. The forests and meadows we could see from the ship were so beautiful that I determined some day to visit Pondo Land.

We were able to enter the mouth of the St. John's River, as the bar was about fourteen feet and we drew but eleven feet of water. When we went ashore we found Port St. John's quite a village. Although the population was small the position of the town, situated as it was in the only easily accessible pass through the hills for many miles, gave promise of greater development. Here a trail passed inland following the banks of the St. John's River and leading into the very heart of South Africa. The people of the port were both native and European.

We put ashore the last of the passengers we had taken aboard at Cape Town, and received fifty natives of various tribes bound for the Cape. I then did some trading for myself and we prepared to up anchor. The weather had grown cooler within the last few days and we realized that we might expect bitter cold winds and rough going before we reached Table Bay. As we sailed southward, I began to figure what I might expect in the way of profits, and I came to the conclusion that if every trip were as successful as this one my gross income for the year would probably exceed ten thousand pounds sterling.

We were out of port but a few hours when the wind began to freshen from the northeast. It sent us racing along with the clouds above us and the whitecaps on either side. We were exhilarated but hardly alarmed as we were running almost ahead of the wind. The natives in their improvised quarters began to grow restless, however. They said:

> 'Uyeze-Umoya,' the storm is coming, see it rise.
> 'Awu-ye-lelema-ma,' woe is coming upon us.

Then one more deep-voiced than the rest brought quiet with his words,

> 'En-gomte-to,' it is the law of God.

The rough weather did not disturb Sydney Wilson. As he moved about the galley getting our evening meal he bellowed a spiritual that could be heard from one end of the ship to the other.

> 'I know Jesus am a medicine man,
> I know Jesus can understan', understan',
> I know Jesus am a plate of gold;
> Gives yo' one swaller and it cures yo' soul.'

Then as the spray from a big wave shot in through the open galley door, he began that mournful chanty,

> 'I don't want to die in the storm dear Lord,
> I don't want to die in the storm . . .'

As the wind began to shift toward the eastward, however, we all grew grave. We mustered the crew at their stations and battened the hatches. The barometer, which had been falling slowly all afternoon, now began to drop with alarming rapidity. Everything was shored and double lashing used. Up to this time the wind had been free and we had been in little danger, but we seemed to have run into the vortex of the storm while trying to avoid it. 'Furl topsail,' I roared. And the first mate, 'Port watch lay aloft. Furl the topsail.' The answer of the port watch as they made their way precariously up the ratlines was blown back into their teeth, yet I could hear, 'Aye, aye, the topsail.' We continued to reef until we were running under nothing but the fore staysail. For perhaps twenty minutes we scudded along ahead of the wind, but as the wind continued to shift toward the east we saw that soon we would be on a lee shore.

'Port the helm!' I shouted. And then a few minutes later, 'Port the helm!' There was nothing for it but to point up into the wind and sail as close to her as we could. To save ourselves we had to run out to sea. Soon the rollers began breaking over the ship, flooding the waist and putting everything awash. Things were as tight as we could make them yet the water came leaking into the galley, the cabin, and the forecastle. I was thankful that I had ordered double tarpaulins placed over the hatches. Now the lightning began to flash and the thunder roar, followed by great bursts of tropical rain. During one flash I could see Braithwaith making his way aft with the greatest difficulty. He finally reached me and shouted in my ear, 'There's danger of a panic among the passengers, sir.'

'Put a watch over them,' I ordered. 'Keep them quiet the best you can.' Those fifty lives caused me great anxiety during the trying hours.

The Pedro Gorino was a weatherly ship and under any sort of sail would gain to windward. In this case, however, we had been forced to reef until she barely held her own. It was little wonder, for we were bucking not only the wind but a strong ocean current that swings around the Cape from the Indian Ocean. Once the helmsman, swept from his feet or fatigued with labor, lost control of the helm. For a moment it felt as though we were tumbling over a building. Then as we fell into the trough of the waves the ship began to shiver and shake as though she would open every joint and seam. We recovered, however, and proceeded to wear ship hour after hour. It was at this point that I became acquainted with the skillful seamanship of Peter Benjamin and the admirable qualities of the Pedro Gorino. The ship was overloaded, the mate tired and harassed, yet both proved to be of such a staunch, unyielding nature that even the onrushing sea in all its mad fury could not quench their courage. Before morning the rain had turned to hail and the wind was bitter cold. We all suffered from the chill, but the natives, who were almost without clothes and in flooded quarters, probably suffered the most.

We had a hard night of it with all hands on deck. The sea ran high and the sky was overcast. But through one small circular opening where there were no clouds at all we were aware of the distant stars and the peaceful sky of midnight blue.

Hour after hour and day after day, we bucked the

wind and the waves. Occasionally we were able to take a half hour's rest on our wet cold bunks, but for the most part we were on duty all of the time. At last, after one of the worst trips in my recollection, we reached Cape Town, battered and bruised and fully aware of what we might expect in our future voyaging in that part of the world.

CHAPTER X

THE PHANTASY AT KNYSNA

ONE afternoon as I sat at my desk in my office on the Strand, two English gentlemen in top hats entered. Although I had never seen them before their easy and familiar 'Good afternoon, Captain Dean,' their open manner, and their frank, good-humored faces threw me completely off my guard. They were not only well dressed, they had a perfect Oxford accent, and although I should have realized that my efforts in behalf of the Kid had thrown me in the wrong light with the English and that it was important to be careful, I had no idea that these English gentlemen were on anything but legitimate business. It would have taken a wiser man than I to have foreseen the coming weeks.

Within a few moments they had explained the situation. These two with several of their friends, all young bloods just out from England, had seen all they cared to of the Boer War and thought a little hunting and adventuring along the coast would suit their fancy. They had seen the Pedro Gorino where she lay in the harbor and they had been impressed with her fine lines and rigging. They had set their hearts upon that ship and had come to me to procure her for the hunt.

My business at this time was a profitable one and I was not altogether willing to accept a charter from these young gentlemen. When they asked me how much I would charge for sixty days, I replied, more to cool their ardor than for any other reason, 'Oh, six hundred pounds sterling.' The figure did not seem to faze them. The older of the two took three hundred pounds in notes from a roll in his pocket and passed them across the desk, saying he would pay the rest when the trip was under way. I offered to make out a receipt, but he declined with a wave of his hand. He did not even think it necessary to put our agreement on paper. My word as a gentleman satisfied him completely.

Strangely enough, it seemed to me, these men wanted no crew — a bare-boat charter. They intended to sail the Pedro Gorino and do the work of sailors for the sheer sport of it. They invited me to accompany them as a guest and I was glad to accept their invitation, for my ship was close to my heart and I should have hated to see it sailing out of Table Bay with no one but strangers aboard.

When I told the crew of my new charter, they made ready to leave the boat somewhat sorrowfully. Sydney Wilson in particular mumbled vituperations, and wished woe to all Englishmen on land or on sea. He took great pride in the cleanliness and orderly arrangement of his galley, and it broke his heart to imagine a stranger desecrating his Holy of Holies.

'Ain't no buck of a man goin' cook like Sydney, skipper,' he pleaded.

'I know it, Sydney, but an agreement is an agreement,' I replied.

He was not to be easily convinced. He explained that he knew every pan in the galley. Had he not served faithfully for months? How could an Englishman cook such stews and roasts as the ones he cooked?

He saw at last that he would have to yield, however, and joined the group on the deck who were preparing to go ashore.

The whole crew looked so disconsolate and dejected that I decided to cheer them up. I told them that they would be paid for the next sixty days exactly as if they were aboard the ship and that when the Pedro Gorino returned from her trip they might have their old jobs again. At this their countenances brightened and they went ashore happy.

Early the next morning the nine sporting Englishmen came aboard. They had weapons of all kinds, fishing tackle, leather bags and trunks filled with their wardrobes, and a great array of nautical equipment. The man who had paid me the three hundred pounds on the previous day had a set of eighteen guns with dull blue barrels and hand-carved monogrammed stocks ranging in bore from a .22 to a sixteen-pound .600 fully capable of stopping a bull elephant. He also had a display of admiralty charts from His Majesty's Stationer such as I have never seen in all my sea-going days. Among their equipment were sextants and compasses, binoculars and telescopes, as well as several complicated instruments which were quite new to me.

Contrary to my forebodings, they were fine sailors. They were all dressed in immaculate white duck and they went about their business with the air of men who know the sea. They could clamber up the ratlines to furl a sail with as much ease as any of my colored boys, meanwhile carrying on a sophisticated and witty conversation.

It was the warm season of the year and we had fine

weather. They had planned to make Knysna their first stop, but instead of plotting a course straight for their destination they sailed the boat capriciously, tacking in and out of the wind for the mere sport of it. The Pedro Gorino, much to my satisfaction, performed in splendid fashion.

When we had been at sea a day or two, however, they began to take less interest in sailing and began playing cards and drinking champagne as young English gentlemen will. The servant they had brought along as cook, steward, and valet was kept busy bringing ice and bottles. They began keeping their watches less regularly, and watching their charts less closely. I hesitated to interfere, but I was greatly relieved when on the fifth evening out of Cape Town we sighted the Heads which guard the entrance to the inner harbor at Knysna.

Knysna itself is some three miles from the sea on a perfectly protected estuary fed by the Knysna River. The depth of water on the bar was easily sufficient to admit the Pedro Gorino and I suggested sailing her into the harbor so that we might be protected from any sudden storm that might arise. It seemed to me that the Englishmen resented my suggestion and more to assert themselves than because of the fast-falling darkness they dropped anchor a mile from the Heads in the almost unprotected sea.

The night was so warm that we slung our hammocks on the deck to catch whatever breeze might be stirring. When I rolled in at midnight the Englishmen were still drinking and playing cards. The sky was cloudy and there seemed little danger of a high wind.

As I fell to sleep I had no premonition that this evening was to be one of the most eventful of my life. . . .

It may have been an hour, although it seemed no such length of time, when I felt myself hurtling bodily through the air. When I fully awoke I was plunging through cold water all entangled in my hammock. In that brief moment a thousand things rushed through my brain. I realized that I was overboard, but how or why I did not know. I realized that I must be near the ship, but the absolute blackness of sea and sky prevented me from seeing anything at all. I called loudly to let the men aboard know that I was in the sea. There was no answer out of the darkness.

The ocean was as silent and as smooth as a pool. Its quiet soothed my nerves and cleared my brain. If one should swim in ever increasing circles, I reasoned, one could eventually locate any object, provided the object was not moving. I began circling around and around and around, thinking on each turn, 'Surely this time.' But after a half hour's fruitless search I had to admit defeat. Deep within me I knew that she was within a few hundred yards, but somehow I had missed her.

I had been a fine swimmer in my earlier days, able to swim as much as six miles in the surf, so I had no fear on that score. But the terrible silence, the way the ship had vanished, and the mystery surrounding my plunge overboard froze the blood in my veins. The sharks were an additional cause for apprehension. On other trips through these waters I had watched them sport fearlessly about the ship and I knew how deadly they were.

For a time I continued to swim and call, but finally

seeing how futile it was I decided to strike out for shore.
The pitch black sky precluded any possibility of learning my directions from the heavens. My swimming in
circles had entirely puzzled the intuitive sense usually
with the mariner. I knew that the shore was less than a
mile away yet I had no way of knowing in which direction. I merely took a chance and struck out. I have no
idea how long I swam. My arms pulled me forward
with monotonous strokes. For ever so long I did not
tire. But as I swam farther and farther, perhaps a mile,
two miles, three miles, perhaps an hour, two hours,
three hours, the sickening thought occurred again and
again, 'Perhaps I am swimming out to sea.' And then
as if all the heavens and seas were plotting against me I
would think, 'Perhaps the shore is but a dozen strokes
away.' I do not know when I tired. I had lost all sense
of time and space. I only know that when I could swim
no more I began to tread water and float by turns. I
began to call again, but my voice was so weak and faint
on the measureless ocean that I soon ceased. I thought
of the great depth beneath me and the other men
asleep on the sea floor. And I remembered a song from
Shakespeare I had learned as a child:

> 'Full fathom five thy father lies;
>   Of his bones are coral made;
> Those are pearls that were his eyes:
>   Nothing of him that doth fade
> But doth suffer a sea-change
> Into something rich and strange. . . .'

The words were infinitely soothing. I became very
drowsy and lost consciousness. . . .

When I awoke I was lying on a sand beach where I

had been washed I have no idea in what manner. The shallow water lay about me to my waist, but my head and shoulders were on the sand in the bright sunlight. In my first amazement I could remember nothing that had gone before. I did not care to move but lay like driftwood tossed upon the beach after a storm. I thought that I must be dreaming, for the sea gulls wheeled and fell about me without fright. Or perhaps I was dead and drowned. The thought filled me with a great sadness.

Slowly the events of the previous evening came back to me. I was aware of a dull throbbing in my head as if I had been severely beaten. I could hear and see in a dreamy sort of way, but none of my muscles would move at my command. My legs seemed rigid and frozen and my arms lay stiffly at my side. I attempted to rise out of the water, but my body refused to move. I tried to shout, but no sound came from my lips.

Perhaps it was minutes or perhaps hours when far off down the beach I saw two figures approaching. As they came nearer I could make out nets upon their shoulders and I knew that they were Africando fishermen trudging homeward. Their brown bodies glistened in the sunlight. I tried desperately to call, but the faint sound of my voice could hardly have been heard five yards away. Luckily they saw me in passing and dropping their nets hurried to my side. They took me on their strong shoulders and carried me to their little village.

I was taken to a native hut and laid upon a bed made of a cow hide stretched between two poles. An Africando girl fed me the broth of herbs and hot teas.

Through my dreamy senses she seemed some dusky goddess. She came and went with quiet footsteps and often laid her hand upon my hot forehead. Her skin was the color of Guinea gold and her breasts hung in her scant dress like two golden apples. When she spoke, her words were like music. These people were less real than any I had ever known, the men so strong, the women so comely.

I had many hours to think and to wonder while I was recovering. If this was not all phantasy there were things hard to explain. Why had the Englishmen thrown me overboard? They might have been drunk, but even so, what could have led them to such an act? How had it happened I could not find the ship? There had scarcely been a breath of air over the ocean, surely not enough to move the ship. How had I escaped the sharks in the bay? And above all how had it happened that having fallen unconscious, I had not drowned but had somehow reached the beach? The currents along those shores are such that the undertow would carry one toward rather than away from the land, yet if I had been swimming out to sea hour after hour I must have reached a point miles from shore before I at last lost consciousness. There was, of course, the possibility that I had been swimming in a circle and had at last approached the beach. No, it was easier to doubt the whole affair. It was all a dream from which I would awake safe aboard my ship.

The Africandos rubbed my body with oil. It was very soothing and seemed to help me regain my strength. My speech returned slowly and with it a limited use of my arms and legs. One day perhaps a week after I had been carried to the hut I tried to rise to my feet. For a moment I stood dizzy and reeling by the side of my bed, then fell backward in a faint.

Minutes seemed hours, hours days. It seemed as if the whole summer had passed before I was at last able to move my tired body out to the sunshine of the beach. I had been a strong and able seaman when I had left Cape Town; now I was more like an image of death than a living human being. My body was emaciated and bent. My beard, never heavy, was yet sufficiently grown to change the looks of my face until an old friend would hardly have recognized me.

As soon as it was humanly possible I prepared to leave for Knysna, some five miles from the fishing village. I had only my pajama trousers, no other clothes of any kind. But clothes matter little in that part of the world, and I started off afoot with two of the Africandos, anxious to learn the truth and recover my ship if it were not already too late. I did not forget to thank the kind people, particularly the girl who had nursed me to health.

When I arrived at Knysna, I commenced inquiring about the Pedro Gorino. No one had seen her. At last I found a man who said that some weeks before he had seen a sailing vessel anchored a mile off the Heads that might answer to my description of the Pedro Gorino, but she had dropped anchor late one afternoon and had been gone by morning. To add to my perplexity not one of my old friends at Knysna recognized me. I went to the dock and the offices of ships' agents, but everywhere I was taken for some old beach comber or beggar. One and all discredited my story. I began to remember stories of men who had come back to earth in other forms. I felt confused, bewildered and lost. Was I really so different from what I had been?

Not the least phantastic of this strange sequence of events was the time involved. The Pedro Gorino had dropped anchor off the Heads on the evening of January fifth. When I reached Kynsna after my convalescence it was January twentieth. I could hardly believe the calendar. What had seemed a whole season was but half a month of summer.

I decided to determine my sanity. Borrowing enough money from the friendly Africandos to wire Cape Town, I sent a message to Peter Benjamin concerning the Pedro Gorino. His return wire stated that she was riding at anchor in Table Bay and had been for the last ten days. I no longer could distinguish the real from the unreal nor the truth from the fabric and weave of my fevered mind. My waking hours were filled with dreams, and at night my dreams echoed my waking hours.

One morning, however, I took new hope. A ship belonging to Thesen and Company had just dropped anchor in the estuary. I went aboard half hoping and half fearing to meet some one I knew. As luck would have it the second mate was one of the men who had come aboard the Pedro Gorino when she had first dropped anchor in Table Bay some months before. He looked at me without a gleam of recognition in his eyes.

'Surely you remember me, Johnson,' I said.

At the sound of my voice his face brightened. 'You're Captain Dean of the Pedro Gorino.'

The ship was bound for Delagoa Bay and was not due to return to Cape Town for some months, so it was impossible for me to take passage aboard her. The officers, however, were a fine sort and lent me fifty pounds. With this I paid my friends the Africandos for their kindness, bought myself clothes, and started by Cape Cart on my journey to Cape Town. Because I was still weak I took the trip by easy stages.

When I arrived at Cape Town my friends listened to my story in amazement. They had seen nothing of the nine Englishmen. Most of them did not even know that the boat had left the harbor, for although I had been gone for over a month, during the last three weeks of that time the Pedro Gorino had lain in Table Bay. My crew went back aboard the ship and trade went on as usual, but for months I carried on an investigation attempting to discover my malefactors. I went to all the authorities but none could or would help me. All that ever came of the affair was a short, semi-humorous article in one of the local papers that took it all as the fabrication of an old salt which might entertain their not-too-serious readers.

CHAPTER XI

LORENÇO MARQUES FOR A SONG

WHEN I was introduced to Senhor De Costa I was only aware that I had met a small, sharp-eyed Portuguese merchant, not at all conscious of the fact that through his subsequent action I might find myself on the verge of making history.

De Costa had come to Cape Town to purchase freight for Delagoa Bay. When I met him he had gathered together several hundred tons. He could easily have chartered a ship large enough to transport all his purchases. Instead, although I could carry less than half of his freight, he offered me a full cargo and thirty native passengers at a handsome figure. I accepted the charter and ordered Benjamin to prepare to receive the freight and passengers. In due course of time I gave the command to up anchor, and we made our departure for Delagoa Bay. As we left Cape Town we noticed over Table Mountain a tablecloth, a cloud perhaps a half mile in diameter. As every mariner in those waters will tell you, it is a sign indicative of uncertain weather. As I had expected, the sea was rough, and I had to plot a wide course to miss Cape Agulhas. We could only use topsails and the forestaysail during the first two days as the headwinds made us run on our starboard beam.

Off the coast of Natal the weather moderated. From here on the sailing was beautiful. Fortunately, every one aboard was inured to the sea, and since there were no women or children we had no sickness. The gull-like qualities of the Pedro Gorino seemed very apparent to me on this trip and I was very proud of my boat.

Much as I liked her performance, however, I began to see that within the next year or so, I would have to install power. I had put it off time and again for sentimental reasons. I had been aboard sailing vessels all my life and I liked the excitement aroused in the fight with wind and weather. It seemed a little sacrilegious and immoral to cheat the ship out of her heritage, but I was convinced that it must be done. Thesen and Company had shown me correspondence from a Rotterdam shipbuilding concern that led me to believe that sufficient progress had been made to revolutionize maritime activities to the extent of making strictly sail obsolete. My exchequer at this time would easily have permitted the change and I was determined to purchase and install a modern power-plant in the very next slack season.

A day or two before we had made our departure, Senhor De Costa had taken the British Mail steamer for Delagoa Bay. His business was pressing and he could scarcely have afforded the slower passage on the Pedro Gorino. At last, with no untoward experiences except a little rough weather and the ordinary humdrum of a voyage on a tropical sea, we sighted Delagoa Bay. Benjamin knew this harbor well and wanted to pilot us into the fairway, but I thought discretion the better part of valor and dropping anchor outside the reefs signaled for a pilot. We were soon in the spacious bay in front of a little city of perhaps five thousand inhabitants, a port with all the earmarks of a Portuguese town.

Lorenço Marques had grown and changed wonderfully since I had seen it as a boy, years before. I found it to be a real African, tropical town and although the majority of the inhabitants were Portuguese or of Portuguese descent, there were also Parsees, Persians, Gypsies, Arabs, Indians, Madagascans, Somalis, English, Boers, Chinese, Japanese, and a motley crew of mixed mulattoes.

At the invitation of Senhor De Costa I came ashore as his guest, and remained with him during my whole stay at Delagoa Bay, leaving the boat in charge of Benjamin. I gave him the responsibility of lightering the freight ashore and releasing the passengers. I realized that there was something unusual in the air and I wanted to be able to apply all my time and energy on the problem when its nature became apparent.

The first sure sign that I had was the attitude of the authorities toward me. Senhor De Costa was a close friend of the Governor, yet this in itself was not sufficient to account for the deference with which the whole staff of government officials treated me. I pretended to enjoy the affairs to which I was invited and I accepted the hospitality offered me as nonchalantly as possible. But the fact remained that I was apprehensive.

My host did his utmost to impress me with the town. He pointed out its fine plaza where business was transacted. He extolled the extreme gentleness of the people who, despite the fact they were a mixed populace, stood in need of very little law enforcement. He showed me how well the various groups mixed in their social and commercial life — for with the exception of the Boers and the English whose political sympathies at this time made them stand aloof, the inhabitants were friendly and congenial. Above all he wanted me to understand the great future ahead of the town. As capital, or at least the seat of the colonial officials who ruled Portuguese East Africa, its position was important and unique.

It was like a game. With a sixth sense, I perceived an ulterior motive, yet I was quite unable to decipher the meaning of the moves De Costa was making.

One of my idiosyncrasies when I have a problem is to walk in the open air while I am trying to solve it. I went everywhere in the little city and was soon acquainted with most of its streets. But I grew to know something more than its physical nature. I had had enough experience with men to analyze predominant emotion when I felt it in the air. I had been in towns, where without a word of actual warning I could sense revolution. Here it was something even more terrible than revolt, it was the feeling of fear. People were glancing nervously toward the bay or back toward the jungle. They talked together and there was fear in their voices. Stupidly enough I was unable to fathom the cause or meaning of their fright until one afternoon, almost by accident it would seem, I met the secretary to the Governor-General.

As we sat at our little table in the shade of two great trees sipping wine we talked carelessly it would appear, yet each to his own purpose. He had lived in the United States for some years. We talked of Philadelphia, Washington, Boston, and New York. Slowly and very naturally the conversation shifted to the colored race in America. He pointed out facts of which I was already painfully aware, particularly that America was no place for the colored race, that as long as the African stayed in that environment he was ruining himself for the more important things in life; he was lessening his own chances of ever gaining social prestige or political independence, and he was encountering a climate and a culture devastating to his morals and his intellect. To all this I readily agreed, wondering meanwhile why this Portuguese Government official should suddenly become so eloquent upon a problem that while it concerned me more deeply than any other problem in the world had no reason whatsoever for concerning him.

I had always been convinced that the Ethiopian must return to Africa if his race was ever to reach world prominence, but whether or not the secretary to the Governor was aware of my sympathies, he spent a whole hour trying to convince me of my own hypothesis.

Then he switched rather abruptly to the beauties of Delagoa Bay and the great unexploited wealth that lay in the thousands of square miles included in Portuguese East Africa. He grew almost oratorical in his praise of the fine port, the plaza, the prosperity of the province, Lorenço Marques with its view of sea and forest. Finally he came to the point. Leaning more closely than he had hitherto leaned, he almost whispered in my ear, 'I suppose you realize that your position in Africa is as insecure as it is unique.'

I was genuinely puzzled.

'Yes,' he continued, 'we realize that America has one very subtle and powerful influence that no other country can boast. But as long as her agents have no real foothold they are no more secure than the agents of any other country. The penalty for spies is death.'

I asked him to explain himself, and he, thinking that I too was playing the game, complied.

'Of course you understand that we have been watching your movements up and down the coast, your stops at Pondo Land, East London, and Port Elizabeth. Your search is ended. I offer you the opportunity for which you have been seeking, and I offer it in a way that will make your act seem wholly lawful.'

I tried to cover my amazement. 'Just what is my reputed position in Africa?' I asked. 'And what have I been attempting outside of my lawful business in the coast trade?'

'Every one knows,' he told me, 'that you are an intelligence officer in the employ of the American Government and one of the most dangerous sort, since your power over the native is tremendously increased because of your color. As for the immediate object for which you are striving, that too is well known. You have been seeking an opening for your government, any tiny port or town.'

'I deny every word of it,' I said hotly.

'Perhaps you represent another power, another country, another faction, or let us say an organization of your own people'; he shrugged his shoulders, 'the situation remains primarily the same.'

I saw clearly now, and my reply was evasive as I knew it must be.

His voice dropped to a whisper. 'I am offering you the vast territory of Portuguese East Africa including the city of Lorenço Marques for the ridiculously low figure of fifty thousand pounds sterling.'

The possibilities opened before me like a flower: Delagoa Bay, future maritime headquarters for native Africa; Lorenço Marques, a new center of culture for the colored race; Portuguese East Africa, a national home to which the wandering Ethiopians the world over might come and live in peace. Who could tell? With such a foothold an enterprising colony might expand until it had recaptured the whole continent. 'Give me six months,' I said.

He was running his slender hands nervously through his long black hair. 'Impossible, why the . . . why, anything might happen in six months.'

'What might happen within six months?'

'Anything,' he said. But I knew that I had hit at the root of the matter and I determined to investigate a theory of my own the minute that I reached Cape Town.

CHAPTER XII

I LEARN INTRIGUE AT A BITTER SCHOOL

THE next morning I wrote a dozen letters to people of my own race, friends in America and in Europe. I outlined the proposed purchase as glamorously as possible, trying to arouse in others some of the enthusiasm which I myself felt. My plea was for financial and moral support, and I asked my friends to answer immediately and to direct their letters to Cape Town. Fortunately a British Mail steamer was in the harbor and by evening my epistles were on their way.

I was anxious to return to Cape Town, and as I had accepted a charter from De Costa for cargo consigned to Freighter and Elliott the ship was soon loaded and ready to up anchor. I hardly remember the trip, my mind was so filled with Lorenço Marques and the possibilities of an Ethiopian Empire. When we reached Table Bay I left the ship, not to go aboard for many weeks. Captain Peter Benjamin was a perfectly reliable man fully capable of handling all trading operations. I left the boat in his hands.

At Cape Town my attention was for a short time diverted into another channel. Haji Hassan's grapevine intelligence system, of which Hamid Abdurraman was one tendril, reached even into the prison camp on the Breakwater. Thus Hamid had learned that Kid Gardener was in new trouble. He came to me for help and together we plotted and planned how we might help our old friend the Kid.

The class distinctions and stratifications when I was in Cape Town were so numerous as to be utterly bewildering. The British, Hollanders, Portuguese, Spanish, Americans, and Boers were considered Caucasian, although there was plenty of dark blood admixed with most of them. The Africandos, Malays, Cape Colored, Bustards, and Swartz were considered Ethiopian, although much European blood ran in their veins. Race distinction was by rule, and out of this arbitrary ruling grew the oppression necessary to maintain such a structure.

The Kid, because he was an American and fairly light colored, had been quartered in a big open enclosure together with several European prisoners. These men were highly insulted and awaited their chance to taunt the Kid. The prisoners cooked their meals in big iron kettles over an open fire. One day at meal-time a big greasy Boer threw a slighting remark at the Kid and his race. The Texan true to form grabbed the kettle from the fire and hit the Boer over the head. There were two points on which the Kid was touchy. One was his personal honor, the other the honor of his race.

He had been put into solitary confinement by the prison officials and Hamid wanted me to do what I could.

I had only one avenue of hope. It seemed to me that Lord Milner, if approached directly, might start an investigation of prison conditions and secure legislation against some of the worst evils on the Breakwater. Incidentally, he might be able to help Kid Gardener. I realized, however, that the circumstan-

tial evidence was all against the Kid. He and I were
both fighting for race equality, but his demonstrations
were of such a violent nature that it was little wonder
the officials suspected the idealism of his motives.

I took the question to Lord Milner. He heard me
through and promised to do whatever he could. I
doubt if it was worth the effort, however. Shortly
afterward Hamid brought me word that the Kid was
out of solitary confinement; but that, no doubt, was in
the ordinary course of events and not due to anything
I had done or said. Perhaps a year later the whole
prison system was given a severe shake-up, but I have
reason to believe that Lord Milner had only a small
part in that reform.

The only certain result of the whole affair was to
make the English more than ever my enemies. Any
one who turns a hand to help a colored man in South
Africa is suspected of sympathizing with the so-called
'Ethiopian Movement.' Certainly the officials distrusted me and I have been told that some years later
in London, Sir Harry Johnson spoke of me as the most
dangerous 'negro' in the world and a menace to the
peaceful subjugation of the natives in Africa, but that
was after I had gone to visit Segow Faku, King of the
Pondos.

There is no doubt in my mind that the English had
wind of the proposed sale of Portuguese East Africa,
for I was being watched at every turn. But strange to
say it was an Englishman who gave me just the information I was seeking in regard to that purchase. It
was all quite by accident, however, and unintentional
on his part.

There was in Cape Town at this time a very fashionable resort to which the élite came to take the baths. Something about the water was supposed to cure them of all their ailments and like the magical fount of Ponce de Leon bring youth to those who drank and bathed. Here I had seen or met in a casual and informal way most of the notables of Cape Town. One of the most frequent visitors was a portly, bull-necked, ordinary looking Englishman whom I finally discovered to be Cecil Rhodes. Not only government officials, but also officers of the army and navy gathered here.

Shortly after my return from Delagoa Bay while my head was still filled with the prospect of buying the colony the moment I received sufficient backing, and while I was still pondering why the Portuguese should be anxious to sell at such a ridiculously low figure, the whole matter was explained to me, almost as miraculously as if the stars had spoken.

One day I had gone to the bath, and having bathed was sitting in the luxurious lounge. Other frequenters were scattered here and there throughout the great room talking and smoking. As I sat by myself deep in thought I was approached by a man who by his dress proclaimed himself an officer in the English Army. We were soon conversing on this subject and that, including everything from bull-fighting to poetry. On almost everything we disagreed, and when our conversation took the inevitable turn to the Boer War I felt sufficiently argumentative to pretend I was pro-Boer.

I have never been sure whether he was a man planted for the purpose of leading me into a confession concerning Lorenço Marques, or merely a man made indiscreet by anger. Perhaps he had been drinking. But whatever it was that loosened his tongue I am sure that the information he gave me would have constituted evidence for his court-martial.

I argued that the Boers knew the country in a way that the English would never know it, they knew each kopje, and ravine, each drift in stream and river. I tried to show how a mere handful of Boers could harass a whole British regiment. 'You English don't know anything more about guerrilla warfare than you did a hundred and fifty years ago fighting the French and the Indians,' I taunted. 'You're too bull-headed to learn.'

Naturally the officer was angered. 'What do *you* know about war?' he asked, his voice low and tense. 'We will have Paul Kruger on his knees within three months.'

'Just how?' I asked.

Then it was that he outlined a plan, never carried into effect, and long since carefully forgotten. It was a plan to flank the Boers via Delagoa Bay. Five or six men-of-war and transports were to speed to Lorenço Marques and land an army. These English regiments were to march right across the neutral Portuguese territory, and while the army in Cape Colony kept the Boers occupied from the southward, this detachment was to fall upon them from the rear and cut them to pieces before they could fully realize what was happening. In its violation of neutral territory it would have been not unlike the plan pursued by the Germans during the late war.

The crystal cleared and I could see the motives of men and of nations more clearly than as if they had been before me on the printed page. I had, through no virtue of my own, discovered at its inception such a maze of plotting and scheming as a historian may unravel only after years of unprejudiced study, and perhaps not then, for who knows what black secrets lie hidden in the archives of nations.

I could now decipher words that formerly had no meaning. The reason why Lorenço Marques was chill with fear was obvious. They either knew or suspected that the English were preparing to make some such move and they were bending all their efforts toward selling Lorenço Marques before it could happen. They also must have realized that if the Boers learned of the plans of the English they would send an army to prevent the English from landing. In all events the Portuguese knew that they stood in danger of foreign invasion. It was clear why I was being watched by the English. While there was some danger attached to marching through Portuguese territory, it was nothing to the danger of marching across the same country if it belonged to an American citizen. The Portuguese had realized that the title to their territory was not worth a fraction of the total value of their private property, and they had offered me their country not because they wished to lose it but because they wished to keep it.

I realized as thoroughly as any one else how safe the land would be if I could make the purchase, and this new information, rather than discouraging me, urged me to even greater efforts. I sent more letters and planned day and night how I might secure the backing I needed. I would gladly have sold everything I owned, even my beloved ship if it would have brought even a quarter of the necessary funds. It was useless to think of it. I knew that I needed help and hoped against hope that some one of those to whom I had written would be moved by the same high fire that had moved me and, seeing the great possibilities of the future, would give me backing.

As the weeks passed, answers to my letters began to straggle in. Each that I opened brought disappointment. There were men among those to whom I had written who could have forwarded the whole sum yet not one offered so much as a penny. They had forgotten their motherland as completely as if their forbears had not spent their lives in her jungles.

To one hope I clung with tenacity. If all else failed me, I could at least depend upon Captain Forbes. But I hesitated to ask him for help. He had given me more than he could afford already and I realized that while he would willingly procure me the sum I needed he would have to impoverish himself to do it. In my extremity, however, I was almost prepared to ask him to make the sacrifice. Who can foretell the ironies of fate? On the very day I determined to write to him unfolding everything, word came from England of his death. This loss together with my continual disappointments from other quarters went far toward disheartening me, and I began to despair of ever acquiring for my race the territory of Portuguese East Africa.

Thus the bright bubble burst, and the greatest chance the 'negro' has ever had to rehabilitate Africa came to nothing. Every prominent Ethiopian in America had been approached. Without exception they tried to dissuade me. They did not realize that before their eyes, within the reach of their hands, was a possibility to return to their own motherland, to return to the only environment in the world that fits the needs of the colored man, body, mind and soul. They did not realize that for the first time in thousands of years Africa had a chance of arising to her old glory.

Why did you not respond, men of my race? You did not respond because you were born in a land where the Caucasian is in power and the Ethiopian can only imitate. You did not respond because of the centuries during which you have labored under the hypnotic influence of false ideals, false logic, false education, and false code of morals. You did not respond because the spirit had been beaten and whipped from your black bodies until you could no longer hold up your heads.

Did you not realize that a race cannot be freed by others but must free itself?

In your blindness and rustic unsophistication you reminded me of the native Somali, who if you were to offer him a thousand bright gold sovereigns for a quart of goat's milk would refuse, but if you were to offer him three cents' worth of shell money would gladly sell it.

CHAPTER XIII

WE HUNT FOR SEAL AND WHALE IN
THE STRAITS OF MOZAMBIQUE

The merchant with affright, aghast
When Africus with furious blast
Lashes the Icarian waves to foam,
Extols his quiet inland home;
But safe in port he straight equips
Anew his tempest-battered ships,
By no disaster to be taught
Contentment with a lowly lot.

From HORACE

I WAS happy to go aboard the Pedro Gorino once more. It seemed to me that the sea would bring rest to my tired mind and help me to forget my disappointment. Benjamin and Braithwaith had made two successful trips carrying fiber and skins as well as miscellaneous cargo. Their talk, however, was not of trade; it was centered on whaling and sealing, for they had sighted a school of humpback whales on their last voyage. They wanted to fit up the Pedro Gorino as a whaler and set sail for the Straits of Mozambique. It sounded as if it might be good sport so I let them have their way.

When I told Freighter and Elliott of our proposed trip they were enthusiastic and willing to help me all that they could because they had more orders for whale-oil, whalebone, and sealskins than they could fill. When they also realized that on each trip we could do a certain amount of freighting to Delagoa Bay and thus help them to build up their Portuguese trade, they were willing to fit out the Pedro Gorino for her new work at their own expense.

They made me a present of two new whaling boats, gun harpoons, and a great deal of gear for handling and disposing of the whales once we had harpooned them. The whole outfit was new and up-to-date, and we predicted an exciting and lucrative trip.

We accepted freight and passengers for Delagoa Bay and made our departure from Cape Town. The weather was warm with favorable winds. We sailed north and east day after day circling farther and farther to the northward. There was little work to do and much time for singing and story-telling. The whole crew were like boys on a holiday because of the anticipated hunt. I determined to be happy in spite of myself, and threw my whole heart into the work and play about me. Will Braithwaith, Sydney Wilson, and Peter Benjamin shared my cabin with me. They were the greatest trio for singing chanties and spirituals I have ever known. That rhythm! That mournful melody!

> 'Way down yonder by myself
> I couldn't hear nobody pray.
> I couldn't hear nobody pray,
> I couldn't hear nobody pray.
> Way down yonder by myself
> I couldn't hear nobody pray.'

Then Sydney Wilson an octave lower:

> 'I'm goin' to get shot all to pieces
> 'Bout de girl I love . . .'

Who taught you to sing like that, brothers? Sons of

Ham, dark brown bucks born under Scorpio, sing, laugh, be happy. I spent my life in sorrow and what has it profited me? I wish I were back there with you. I would sing too, sing and stamp my feet.

> ' Who built the ark?
> Noah, Noah.
> Who built the ark?
> Brother Noah built the ark. . . .'

Before we realized it we were at Delagoa Bay.

De Costa and two government officials met me at the dock and took me aside to ask me about my progress in securing permission to purchase Portuguese East Africa. They had no idea that it was lack of funds that held me in check. I still had hopes that I could secure backing from some quarter. Perhaps if my trading operations continued to be successful I could swing the deal myself at some time in the future. My replies to their questions were evasive. I knew that my words did not satisfy them, but neither did they completely blast their hopes.

While I was still a prospective buyer they were willing to do anything to help me. And so when they discovered that I wanted a pilot they secured two of the best Portuguese in the port to aid me on my trip through the Straits of Mozambique. These two men knew the Indian Ocean as no others I have ever met, and handled the ship as if they had been aboard her for years.

When we at last made our departure from Delagoa Bay and got off shore of the reefs we ran into the teeth of a wind which was so strong as to make us change our course and run due east. The weather was very bad for three or four days and we were blown this way and that. We were unable to make a fix as the cloudy heavens obscured the stars and moon and sun and there were no points which we could shoot for our latitude and longitude. Finally one night we got sight of Cepheus and got our bearings. We found that we were far south of Madagascar, and since the weather was clearing and the wind shifting we now were able to shape our course northward toward Cape Ste. Marie, the southernmost point of Madagascar. We were now in waters where we might sight whale at any hour, and I gave orders for the watch in the crow's nest to keep a sharp lookout.

By the time we sighted Cape Ste. Marie the weather was very good. We commenced to sail between reefs and little desert islands in as romantic a sea as one could ask. The Portuguese knew the coast well, but we threw the lead for precaution's sake wherever we passed near islands.

The sailor who had been given this task shouted, 'Watch ho,' with each heave, and his voice was carried aft through the clear air.

The islands themselves were very small and for the most part barren, or at best covered with scant vegetation. Some of these islands had coves and the lookout was instructed to keep a sharp watch for any sign of life. It was about six bells in the morning after we had been sailing along this type of coast for some hours that the lookout sighted seal on one of the little islands on our starboard bow. We dropped anchor and prepared to lower two boats. The sea was so still that we could hear the occasional roar of the bull seals where they lay on the opposite side of the island. Because of the intervening jagged heaps of rock we could not see the seals from the deck, but the lookout told us that there were several hundred of them sunning themselves on the shore and swimming in the rocky cove.

I was anxious to see the sport, so I accompanied the party of ten men who manned the boats and proceeded with muffled oars to approach the lee side of the island. We were careful not to make a sound, for if seals are alarmed they slip quickly into the sea and swim to safety. When we reached the shore we pulled the boats up onto the narrow sandy beach and prepared to proceed on foot.

Each of us was armed with a knobkerrie, a South African club-like weapon some three feet long. These we gripped firmly as we proceeded to crawl over rock and sand toward the cove. As we came over a little rise we saw before us the whole colony lying in the sun and swimming in the clear water. There were big bull seals and mother seals with their babies, all unaware of the sudden destruction about to descend upon them. Then one of our men accidentally loosened a little stone, which went leaping and clattering down toward the cove. The spell was broken and the seals went plunging and sliding into the sea, and we came down upon them striking left and right and killing the sleek animals by the dozens. Yet to every one we killed ten slipped away to safety. There were perhaps seventy-five lying dead when we had finished. We had spared the very small seals and we had been able to kill only two or three of the big bulls; those we had captured were mostly females and young males.

The skins are not as fine as the skins of several other varieties of seals that may be taken in other parts of the world, but when plucked and prepared even these will bring a considerable sum in the larger cities of Europe and America. Benjamin and Braithwaith as well as the crew were elated with our first haul. Often a whole colony will swim to safety, so the seventy-five we had killed were quite a bag. The skins were carefully removed, salted, and packed away in puncheons in the hold.

This seemed poor sport to me. There was money in it, no doubt, but I found little excitement in clubbing to death beasts as mild-natured as dogs. Therefore at the next two islands on which we sighted seal I stayed aboard the ship and let the crew do the killing. The next time we dropped anchor we took fifteen, and at the third island which was well up the coast toward the Bay of St. Augustine we took sixty, making a total of about a hundred and fifty seals in the three stops. We had over two puncheons full of valuable skins. These were all that we took, however, partly because I did not like the business and partly because our attention was mainly on whales.

Some of the men tried eating the seal meat but I thought it quite rank.

We sighted St. Augustine Bay early one morning, and before the day was over were well up the coast of Madagascar toward Tulcar. We dropped anchor at this little port and found it to be a town of some thousand inhabitants. The country about the town was beautiful with hills, easy slopes, and green vegetation. The large meadow-like expanses dotted at intervals with clumps of trees and watered by occasional streams reminded me of Natal and some parts of Pondo Land. The inhabitants of this country were for the most part 'negroes' and mulattoes, but there were some Arabs, Somalis, Chinese, Japanese, and Hindus.

Shortly after we had dropped anchor the weather had become so rough that we were forced to await an abatement of wind and waves before we could make our departure. We had been detained for over a week when an English freighter loaded with hides, ivory, and mohair berthed a few hundred feet from us. She had just come down the Straits ahead of a stiff breeze and she was the worse for rough weather. I met her captain when he came ashore and we struck up an acquaintanceship. I brought him aboard the Pedro Gorino and when he saw our whaling tackle he said, 'Just ran across a school of humpbacks up the channel Too bad I didn't have your outfit with me.'

That was all that was needed to set the crew wild. Even Benjamin, usually the most calm and cautious of mariners, wanted to put out to sea that night. I was able to convince him that it would be best to wait until morning as the sea was running high. The next morning despite the bad weather we made our departure. For several days we were beating up the Straits of Mozambique first on one tack then on the other, fighting a stiff head-wind all the way. The weather was chilly but bracing. We were all at a high pitch of excitement, anxious to see whale and take our chances at capturing a few big fellows.

We kept a sharp watch, but for nearly a week we did

not see a whale. Then as we were about to lose faith our luck changed. Early one morning sailing through a choppy sea we heard the welcome cry from the crow's nest, 'Ahoy, whale on starboard bow.' A few minutes later we could see them from the deck. It was an enormous school of humpback whales, enough whalebone and whale-oil to make a man rich.

'All hands, ahoy,' I shouted. Peter Benjamin put his head down the booby-hatch and repeated my order. The men scrambled to the deck ready for the sport and greatly surprised at the number of whales on our starboard. I now gave Peter Benjamin command of the ship as he was an old and experienced whaler. We sailed as near as we dared and then dropped anchor. His orders were not shouted now. 'Stand by for whaleboat,' he said to his watch. Then quietly and quickly he told off the men going in the whaleboats. Braithwaith was to handle the harpoon in one of the boats and Benjamin himself in the other. Each of the boats had four of our best men at the oars. Each had a reliable coxswain. When the two boats were lowered and the six men in each had taken their places, they proceeded with muffled oars to approach the school of whales.

Those of us who were left aboard the ship watched the operations with great excitement. The whales were perhaps two hundred yards from us and seemed to be moving leisurely northward. The sea was so rough that I doubted the ability of any man to draw a bead with the harpoon gun, but Braithwaith and Benjamin were old and experienced whalers and had shot and thrown the harpoon in both the Pacific and

Indian Oceans. They were not to be discouraged by a little thing like rough weather.

Both men shot at the same instant. First we saw the smoke and a moment later the report came over the water. There was a sudden commotion among the school of whales and most of them were out of sight in a few seconds. We could easily see from the ship's deck that two of them would never again join their more fortunate fellows. Braithwaith had harpooned a fairly small cow and after a fifteen-minute struggle drew his boat alongside his prey and killed it with a well-placed shot.

Peter Benjamin, however, was having a tougher time of it. He had shot his harpoon into the biggest bull of the whole lot. The infuriated mammal rushed the little whaleboat and would have broken it into a hundred pieces had it not been for the ability of the coxswain and the men at the oars, who were able to avoid the rush through great effort and dexterity. Then the whale sounded. It seemed as if nothing but the bottom would stop him as he went down and down. We could see Benjamin playing out the line and we all hoped that he had a sufficient length. At last the whale went no deeper but commenced to run, dragging the boat and its crew rapidly through the rough sea. I gave the command to up anchor and we followed as closely as we could with the Pedro Gorino. We now had Braithwaith's whale in tow, but no one could foretell the outcome of Benjamin's struggle.

At last, however, it became evident that the whale at the bottom of the sea was beginning to tire. A few minutes later the lookout cried, 'There he blows.' This moment was the most perilous of the whole fight, for the great bull rose so perpendicularly that he came to air almost beneath the whalers, and the wave of water from his body threw the men from their seats and the small boat on her gunwale. The men righted the boat, however, and the struggle continued. It must have been a full half-hour later that Benjamin finished him with three shots.

It is inadvisable to tow whales in these waters, as the sharks will soon gather. Now that the excitement was over we were confronted with the job of cutting up the carcasses which had been brought alongside, hoisting the chunks aboard, and reducing the blubber. Sydney Wilson superintended the disagreeable work of rendering the oil and soon the crew were laboring in earnest. It was disillusioning after the thrilling fight which had preceded.

For several reasons I determined to end our whaling. The wind from up the channel continued to blow fitfully, making progress in that direction a long hard fight. Time is precious to a ship owner and he must take such things into consideration. The humpback whales found in this part of the Indian Ocean give only a small percentage of the oil that the so-called right whale gives, and with no such quality or value as the oil taken from the sperm whale. I saw that while whaling was an exciting and adventurous life it could hardly net us half of what a successful year of trading would. Above all I saw that while trading kept me in touch with the natives all along the coast of Africa, whaling precluded any such contacts and therefore was a hindrance to my most important objectives.

We put about and headed for Delagoa Bay, where we were fortunate in securing a full cargo and some dozen or fifteen passengers. With these and our more or less meager supply of sealskins, whale-oil, and whalebone we headed for Cape Town and made a fast trip ahead of a stiff breeze.

BOOK III
SEGOW FAKU, KING OF THE PONDOS

CHAPTER XIV

THE BLACK ARCHANGEL AND HIS SWORD OF FIRE

BISHOP LEVI JENKINS COPPIN, generalissimo in the legions of Christ, and pillar of the African Methodist Episcopal Church, was born the middle of last century on the eastern shore of Maryland to poor but devout parents. At an early age he was apprenticed to a wheelwright, and like his illustrious Master learned the use of tools in shaping wood. While still a child he joined the church, where it was found that he was endowed with the love of God and obsessed with the Holy Ghost.

He was one of the few Afro-American children in his neighborhood who learned to read and write, and before long he was teaching and advising those about him. After he had vanquished the devil on the eastern shore of Maryland he went to Philadelphia intent on new worlds to conquer. Here he met Fannie Jackson, my teacher and my mother's friend. This kind woman devoted her rare talent to his development, helped him to receive a University education and to prepare for the ministry. After his graduation he became the pastor of Bethel Church of precious memory. Thus he spent most of his life in the very cocoon of African Methodism. While pastoring at Bethel, the Reverend Mr. Coppin wrote many books and developed a ripe scholarship because he was in touch with some of the best minds in America at the city of brotherly love.

At forty he married his teacher, Fannie Jackson, who

was easily ten years his senior. She continued to help him with his studies, fully determined to make him a bishop. When at last he was rewarded and elected to the bishopric, the church decided to send him to South Africa to redeem that motley world and to organize a Fourteenth Episcopal District.

On my return from the Straits of Mozambique I learned for the first time of his approaching arrival. I was immediately interested, not only because he was the husband of my old friend and teacher, but because he was coming to aid the natives of South Africa. I determined to arrange for a suitable reception and with this in mind went to my old friend F. Z. S. Peregrino, editor of the *South African Spectator*.

He was more than willing to help me, and we two with the aid of Reverend Mr. Gow, a native clergyman and resident of Cape Town, began to make preparations. We were not the only ones awaiting the Bishop's arrival with interest. The newspapers took note of it as did the English in every station of life. These imperialists, realizing that they held their position through sheer physical power, watched with jealousy those spiritual and intellectual forces threatening their supremacy. They were not sure of his intention or purpose. It is certain that understanding native psychology as they do, they realized that the Bishop's position and type of work held a glamour for the Ethiopian mind, and that were he so inclined he might arouse any one of a half dozen tribes to rebellion. At this time, with the English forces occupied fighting the Boers, such trouble would have been embarrassing. Whatever their line of reasoning it was evident that they were apprehensive and never once underestimated the importance of his arrival.

When the Bishop's boat came into the harbor, six of us met him at the dock. He arrived very unpretentiously without so much as a secretary to help him with his voluminous writing. His voice was rich and clear, somewhere between a tenor and a bass. He had a stature to match his intellect.

The reception was held in one of the better halls of Cape Town. It was attended by two or three thousand people, fully half of whom were Europeans and including in its numbers most of the government officials of Cape Town. Before them on a dais of huge proportion sat the Bishop, six feet tall, dark brown, handsome, his intelligent face radiant with belief. We opened the meeting with song and the Bishop's voice like Gabriel's silver trumpet could be heard above the voices of the entire congregation. Peregrino gave the address of welcome. In reply Bishop Coppin rose, lifted his throne-like seat which must have weighed one hundred and fifty pounds high above his head, and shouted, 'With such strength I have come to lift the impoverished natives of Africa from their lowly state and to crush beneath my heel the so-called Christian who would keep his colored brother in darkness.'

Never since John the Baptist went crying through the wilderness, 'Repent ye: for the Kingdom of Heaven is at hand,' has a man so moved those who heard him. His words penetrated to the very recesses of the dark and ancient forests, awaking the drowsing consciousness of Africa asleep these thousands of years.

More than one Englishman returned to his home convinced of the Bishop's power and secretly uneasy, half fearing the sword of vengeance.

After the reception, the Bishop, Reverend Mr. Gow, and I accompanied Peregrino to his home overlooking the bay. Bishop Coppin was stirred through and through by the reception and by the other experiences of his first days in South Africa. Always a poet and musician, he was moved to write the words to what has since become a famous African Methodist Episcopal Hymn, 'Ethiopia Stretch Forth Thy Hands.' He wrote swiftly for ten or fifteen minutes, then turned to us and read that stirring song which begins:

'Stretch forth thy hands! What though the heathen rage
And fiends of darkness all their wrath engage?
The hand of God still writes upon the wall,
"Thy days are numbered; all the proud shall fall." '

CHAPTER XV

IN THE HANDS OF THE BOERS

WHEN the Bishop discovered my aims and ambitions in Africa he began to realize how much we had in common and our friendship grew daily. One afternoon several weeks after his arrival we were walking through the Gardens. Our conversation turned to the Pondos, and the Bishop asked my advice on a puzzling situation.

Segow Faku, King of the Pondos, had sent a messenger to the Bishop begging for help in building and organizing schools and churches. The King was willing to do anything within his power to help his people, but he had been so impoverished by the imperialists that he was quite unable to accomplish his desired ends. It almost broke Bishop Coppin's heart, for he had neither the means nor the men to help these poor natives.

As we walked I realized that he had reached a solution. 'Brother Dean, has the spirit ever moved you to join a flock?'

I had to admit that it had not.

'Surely you believe in the teachings of Jesus Christ?'

I hesitated a moment before replying that I inclined more toward Buddhism.

This shocked and saddened the good bishop, but he continued, 'Yet if the opportunity offered, you would sacrifice much for your race.'

'I would do anything within my power,' I said.

'Will you leave your business and go to Pondo Land?' I thought a full minute before answering. The Bishop was playing upon a side of my nature which I had always considered the most human: my desire to help my race. There was, on the other hand, my profitable business which might suffer from my absence. 'But why did you come to South Africa?' I asked myself. 'Was it not to help the native?' This no doubt was my big chance; what did business or anything else matter? 'I will go,' I said.

Later in the day we met Emtinso, the ambassador from King Segow Faku. He was a small, wiry native with a fair command of English. He had been doing lay preaching in Pondo Land for the last three or four years, and when the King had chosen him as a messenger to go to Cape Town to see the Bishop, he had been more than willing. Emtinso's greatest desire was to be ordained. The Bishop had complied with this native's wish, several days before the afternoon of our meeting. Emtinso was overjoyed with his new title, and told every one confidentially that he was a Minister of the Gospel.

After we had parted with Emtinso the Bishop said, 'He will be your guide on the trip to Pondo Land. God be with you both.'

I made all my arrangements as quickly as possible. I put my maritime affairs in the hands of Freighter and Elliott. I put Peter Benjamin in charge of the Pedro Gorino with Braithwaith as first mate and gave explicit instructions. With the help of Emtinso, I purchased an outfit for the long trip. I secured credentials from the American Consul and — with great difficulty — a military pass from the British Government, signed by the English commander and the Governor of Cape Colony. Finally, I bought tickets for De Aar and we were ready to begin our journey. At last we boarded a train and were on our way.

It is a little hard to explain why we went to the country of the Pondos overland and at great personal danger, when we could so much more easily have gone around by sea. It is true that Emtinso wished to visit a dozen or more little parishes on the way, but this was scarcely sufficient reason for our journey through disputed country in wartime. It may have been our love for adventure. More probable than either of these is a third explanation. We did not appreciate the dangers of the war. In Cape Town we scarcely knew a war was being waged until De Wet made his advance. Yet De Aar, our present destination, was in danger of attack at any hour. Already the English had discontinued service by railroad beyond this point. Already English troops were gathering to resist the Boers.

We realized that after we reached De Aar we must proceed by trek train in actual danger of capture by the enemy, yet we hardly gave it a second thought. Our only wish was that the train would travel faster. We shared our compartment with a woman of perhaps fifty who had, besides innumerable packages and a jar of marmalade, a big wicker basket full of kittens. Our other companion was a young English army officer. When the conductor came to take our tickets he swore at Emtinso in Cape Dutch and then asked, 'What de hell you doin' in der wid white people, swartz?' Emtinso, being a meek and lowly follower of the Nazarene did not know what to reply.

The woman covered her ears and said, 'Tut, tut, tut.'
The officer said, 'It's all right.'

I shouted, 'What do these tickets entitle us to? Our passage, or your insults?' The kittens hearing the commotion upset their basket and the jar of marmalade. The conductor beat an ignoble retreat.

When we at last disembarked at De Aar, Emtinso took me some distance up one of the little streets to where a man sat at the door of his cottage. After they had greeted each other in the native language Emtinso informed me that this house was to shelter us until we took the trek train. After a dinner of mealies and kid meat we went to view the town.

We found it a very unpretentious village. Its inhabitants included several hundred Europeans, several hundred Cape colored, and a large group of natives. We found a heavy British guard thrown about De Aar with a regiment encamped on the outskirts. Finally we came to a great meadow known as the outspan. Here were numbers of huge covered wagons and many head of sleek oxen. Yokes were lying everywhere. Little, half-naked, Hottentot boys with sjamboks, whips of rhinoceros hide forty feet long, ran here and there urging the oxen. Emtinso introduced me to several of the drivers and the boys about the meadow. Before we left we learned that the trek train for the karoo would leave at daybreak in the morning. We returned to the little house where we had left our luggage, and after another repast of mealies and kid meat we put up for the night.

At the break of day with a great commotion and yelling and cracking of sjamboks, twelve wagons wheeled into line and prepared to take the trail northward across the karoo. The trek men came noisily for our luggage and put it in the wagons. Emtinso and I could have ridden, but since we were now on the high veld the air was brisk and we preferred to walk. I was fascinated with the skill of the drivers. Each of the enormous wagons was drawn by sixteen powerful oxen, eight pairs, making a string well over fifty feet long. At the head of the column was a little native boy of nine or ten who trudged along leading the oxen. The driver on our wagon was so expert that though he was walking at the fore wheel he could snap flies off the ears of oxen well up the line with his long sjambok, and when he wished he could make the whip crack like the report of a gun.

All day long through a dry, dreary and desert-like country the oxen pulled the heavy wagons creaking and groaning through the sand. Up and down hills, across dried up streamlets, through mountain passes and on and on we labored. Nowhere was there a drop of water, only the dry stubble, a sad reminder of the rains months before. No living thing save the mimosa growth and in the vast distance an occasional herd of antelope. These two clung tenaciously to life, the trees sending their roots far down to hidden moisture, the blesbok, and springbuck moving swiftly out of range and disappearing against the protective landscape.

Fortunately we had cool water, for each of us had taken with us a large square canvas bag with a mouthpiece at one end. These bags had been filled and hung on the outside of the wagons where the wind had full play upon them. Thus through the slight evaporation which was continually taking place from their surfaces our water was always ice cold.

It was well after dark when we pitched camp for the night. The wagons were drawn into a circle and the oxen were tethered. The boys who had led the oxen gathered brush and lit a fire. Soon the coffee was boiling and the mealies simmering. Those who so desired reclined on their karosses (robes of skins). The guards were posted against hyenas, leopards, or an occasional lion. Within the circle of the wagons the fire lit the faces of our companions. We might have been within a room except that high above us the cold stars sparkled.

The Africandos are good story-tellers and I sat up far into the night listening. Their language which is an admixture of broken English, Dutch, and native words and phrases is at first hard to understand. It has a rough music that holds one's attention even where it cannot be understood. The main difficulty is to catch the individual words, as a whole sentence comes in one breath. The profanity they have picked up from the English is no longer profane but is merely used for emphasis. One of the stories concerning the defeat of a braggart, which threw the Africandos into convulsions of laughter ran something like this:

One hell-ob-a-brawn brain-mawn fight ebery mawn too-dam-mach. He put sack ob impops (mealies, native grain) on back and tell eberybody, 'You lick me, you take impops.' One lazy-mawn hear about.

He say, 'I whip you.' One hell-ob-a-brawn brain-mawn say, 'All right fight you to-morrow mornin', bet-cha-hat Lazy.' Lazy-mawn go to him boy an' tell him, 'Boy, if brain-mawn hit me tree times good lick, run like de debil.' 'All right,' say boy. Next mornin' fight. Hell-ob-a-big-one hit lazy-mawn two good lick, knock down. Lazy-mawn cry, 'Boy, time am come.' Boy say, 'Wait dat no tree good lick. Wait him give you one more.' Brain-mawn say to self, 'Lazy wait me give him one more lick, gonna kill maybe, gotta knife in sterlreim (breech-clout) maybe. Better run.' Hell-ob-a-big-one get scared, run. Leave impop for lazy-mawn.

At the conclusion of this story most of the audience shouted, 'Icoona,' meaning 'It is the truth,' or 'I understand.' One among them, however, cried, 'Ambaguthly,' meaning 'I doubt it,' or 'Go on with you.' His remark was merely a matter of form and really signified that he had a story to tell which he considered infinitely more entertaining. On this particular occasion it was further adventures of the 'brain-mawn.'

It recounted how after he had gone to market and purchased the head of a bull for fifteen shillings the 'brain-mawn' carried his purchase far out on the veld and placed it in the mud so that it seemed as if an entire bull were sunk in the mud with nothing but his head above. Then this wily son of Satan had offered several men who were passing five shillings if they would help him pull his bull out of the mud. The men had pulled and the head had come loose, whereupon the 'brain-mawn' had told them that they would either have to pay him five pounds for killing his bull or come before the magistrate. The people were so frightened that, unbelievable as it may seem, they paid the five pounds.

When I finally rolled up in my kaross it must have been midnight. The karoo was quiet without a wind, the air cool and clear. For a few minutes I lay awake thinking of the nearness of the war and wondering a little at the unconcern of the drivers. Then, since I was very tired and drowsy, I dropped to sleep.

The next morning we were up early. We prepared breakfast before daybreak to the accompaniment of cracking sjamboks and creaking wheels. All through the day we labored through country of the same desert-like nature as the day before. Only one who has crossed this country can realize its dangers and difficulties. Often there were mirages to bewilder the unaccustomed eye and occasionally we came upon long stretches where the trail was completely obliterated. Our drivers, however, were experienced freighters and knew the route well. They made remarkably good time, all things considered.

That evening at dusk we pulled into a small town where we planned to spend the night. We had just succeeded in drawing the wagons into a circle when from every direction mounted men thundered down upon us out of the half-light.

'The Boers,' some one shouted. But it was too late to resist. A Boer detachment under Captain Wessel had occupied the town that very day, and we had driven into the camp of our enemy all unaware of our danger.

Captain Wessel was among us in person. He addressed us in perfect English, 'Your arms, gentlemen.' The drivers, who were badly frightened, complied readily, even hunting for the guns among our luggage. Fortunately they missed my two Colts, my rifle, and my shotgun packed away with my other things in one of the wagons.

Captain Wessel was a man of perhaps forty years of age. He was six feet tall with raven black hair and a strong, hard face. His skin was dark enough so that he would have been taken for a quadroon in America. He was dressed in khaki pants, puttees and short boots of dove-colored buckskin. A bandanna handkerchief about his neck, and a broad-brimmed felt hat like that worn by a Texas cowboy completed the picture. He was armed with a forty-five rifle which was slung across his back, two pistols at his side, and a great cartridge belt around his waist. Satisfied that he had confiscated all our guns, he remounted and rode away with most of his company, leaving twenty mounted men to guard us.

Thus we remained all night, unable to leave our camp under penalty of being shot.

CHAPTER XVI

THEN ON ACROSS SOUTH AFRICA

I awoke before daybreak and in the gray light I was able to see that the guards were still at their posts. My comrades slept soundly, huddled in their karosses. The fires from the previous evening sent up thin wisps of smoke through the motionless air, and all about us loomed the bulky wagons. Somewhere in the distance a cock crew.

'Wessel,' I thought. 'Where have I heard that name before?' Not that it is uncommon in South Africa, but that somewhere in the immediate past it had held significance for me. For a few moments it eluded me, and then as my brain cleared it came in a flash. Wessel in Cape Town. His story of their family of brothers. Their little farm on which diamonds had been discovered. The trickery of the English. Their subsequent poverty and hatred for imperialists. It seemed to me that he had told me of a brother who was a captain among the Boers. What a stroke of luck if this were the man. I hardly dared to hope for such good fortune, but I determined to use my knowledge to the best advantage.

Wessel and his men returned just as the sun was rising. He went through our papers rapidly, stacking them in two piles as if he were dealing hands at cards. When he came to mine he hesitated a moment, read them through more thoroughly and then called me by name.

'Dean,' he said. 'Is Captain Dean here?'

I stepped out from among the others.

'So you are an American Missionary?' he asked.

'Not exactly,' I said. And then I explained the nature of my journey.

'What's happening in Cape Town these days?'

'I suppose you know as well as we that the blue-jackets have landed, and that there are rumors of proclaiming martial law throughout Cape Colony.'

'I must admit I do.'

I decided that the time had come, so I tackled the situation boldly. 'Have you a brother in Cape Town?' I asked. He had. And for the next twenty minutes we were on common ground. This fortunate acquaintanceship I made on the karoo secured for Emtinso and for me the right to proceed unharmed with a full quota of oxen and all our papers. We were very thankful for our deliverance, but our joy was tempered when we found that some of our less fortunate fellows were to be detained.

Of the twelve wagons which headed bravely northward from De Aar six were confiscated, together with more than half the oxen and freight. Our sadly mutilated train set forth a half-hour later on a very different route than we had planned. The drivers were taking no more chances. They were headed for Middelburg as fast as they could drive their tired oxen.

Such an event as the one just related could never have taken place in any recent European war. But in the wholesale guerrilla warfare characterizing the struggle in South Africa almost anything was possible.

Numerous bands of picturesque Boers would harass the English wherever they met them, from behind the kopjes or small hills. Sometimes there was open battle, but much oftener it was a fire-and-run sort of fighting. They had confiscated only what they needed of our train; there seemed to be a rough honor about their procedure. Yet to every chivalrous Boer there were two John Smuts, hating the natives like the Devil hates ,holy water, and killing them like flies whenever the opportunity offered itself.

We had been on the trail less than two hours when we met a British column moving forward to meet the Boers. We reported the confiscation of our wagons and the position of the enemy which caused no little excitement among the English. Wessel's men were De Wet's advance guard, and their proximity meant that an attack from the Boers was imminent. The English were determined to stop any further advance of the wedge driven into Cape Colony. On receiving our information, this column moved rapidly forward toward the scene of our disaster.

After traveling across the karoo until we were quite weary of it, we at last came to Middelburg. Here we joined other wagons and after adding fresh oxen to our depleted and jaded lot proceeded through country more fertile and prosperous than heretofore. Everywhere about us were fields of produce kept green through irrigation. This country was less rugged than some we had seen, but there were many kopjes and sometimes in the distance blue lines of mountains.

As we were traveling less than thirty miles a day we had plenty of time for thought. In three days of dreaming I rebuilt the Ethiopian Empire. In three days of dreaming I recaptured Africa for the Africans. Once more Mashonaland was Ophir, and gleaming black bodies brought gold from the mines. The ruins of Zimbabwe were no longer ruins, but stately masonry. The sons of the ancient race who raised those piles of stone to forgotten gods once more were proud possessors of all they surveyed. And those dark descendants of the Phœnicians, still worshiping the crane and the ram, reattained the genius of their ancestors, sailing their ships to every country, bearing the wealth of Africa. As in the ancient days, precious stones and metals poured from Sheba northward through all Arabia, and westward down the wide rivers of the jungle. Nowhere were there slaves, or poverty, or ignorance. In three days of dreaming I dammed the rivers to water the karoo until the desert bloomed like the rose. I built cities in trackless thickets and from the forests of Africa constructed such a fleet of graceful ships as the world has never seen.

At last we came to the Kei River and crossed it late one evening and made our camp. When we awoke next morning we found ourselves in a beautiful land filled with game and covered with green foliage. Here there were many buck, slender graceful animals of a dozen varieties, mostly buff or brown in color with occasionally markings of black. They were very timid, with large brown eyes, and could be seen grazing in small herds on every hand. They could often be surprised at water holes or run down on horseback, and we had no trouble in securing fresh meat. We fished the streams, bathed in the rivers, and enjoyed this part of our journey greatly. When we came to Idutywa in the middle of the Transkei we took lodgings and rested over Sunday.

Here I met Mary Brandon Tulley, a young colored missionary from Canada. She had married one of the lesser chiefs of the district and had made the Transkei her home. She had established a fine mission and had so modernized the native architecture that I found windows and hard-surfaced floors in all the houses, and a degree of culture among the natives unusual in even the older settlements. She offered us the hospitality of her attractive little home, but as we had made other arrangements we had to decline.

At Idutywa we left the great wagon drawn by oxen which had brought us from De Aar and took the two-wheel Government Cape-cart, which carried both mail and passengers. It was pulled by six mules, and at times we were able to make seven miles an hour. In general we arrived at the various villages and stations on scheduled time. Our driver was a Cape colored. He handled the cart with assurance although the road was often rough and steep. At first Emtinso, the driver, and I were the only occupants, but late the first evening when we stopped at a small town to change mules we were joined by an English colonial magistrate. He was of Dutch descent, and although the cart was made to accommodate six he was so enormous that he took all the remaining room.

Because they were carrying the mail, the Cape-carts traveled all night. Emtinso did not try to sleep but sat awake looking up at the stars. I slept fitfully. But the magistrate snored all night long. Occasionally when the road was particularly rough he would grunt unhappily and mutter, 'Ach vot troubles,' but almost immediately he would recommence his snoring.

When morning came he awoke and began to howl for breakfast. 'Vot? Not at der station yet? My, vot a terrible driver ve got.' The driver hastened to inform him that we were only six miles from the station and that breakfast would surely be ready when we arrived. This assurance brightened the magistrate to such an extent that he decided to have a drink on it, and soon he became voluble in his praise of the scenery. When he found that Emtinso was a preacher he began quoting Scripture. 'Blessed is der man vot trusteth in der Lord. . . .' And on and on and on. After we had listened to him for fifteen minutes we could none of us bear it any longer. I took it upon myself to quiet him. I told him that I could not reconcile Christianity and imperialism, and that the man who preached the one and practiced the other was in my eyes a hypocrite. He was not at all offended by my thrust. On the contrary he winked at me, stopped quoting Scripture, and offered us his bottle.

When we at last reached the post station we found ourselves in a prosperous little village of some hundred and fifty inhabitants. There was a small hotel beside the road and the bell was ringing for breakfast. The enormous Dutchman, smelling the savory odor of cooking, vaulted over the side of the cart with the agility of a boy and outstripped us all in reaching the table.

We four sat down at one table. The Africando waitress called out the bill of fare. The first on the list was fried chicken, and without waiting to hear another word· we all ordered fried chicken. While the girl was in the kitchen getting our orders, the manager, a young English colonial, entered the room. He wished us a good morning pleasantly enough, but upon seeing Emtinso his manner changed and he addressed him sharply in Cape Dutch. Emtinso rose meekly and prepared to leave us.

I said, 'Wait, Emtinso, what did he say?'

'He say, "Black man go eat in kitchen."'

I was so incensed that a mere hotel-keeper should speak in this way to a minister of the cloth that I rose to my feet and looking the Englishman squarely in the eye said, 'I have yet to find a more egotistical people than the English. You may have your choice. Apologize to Emtinso, or answer to me.'

The Englishman was taken aback, but game. He was all for trial by combat. At this point, however, the magistrate stepped in. He said to the hotel-keeper, 'Apologize to him. Sure ting apologize to him. I vill advise dem to bring charges against you if you vill not apologize.'

The Englishman, seeing that his license might be endangered, bowed ever so slightly to Emtinso and said with a sneer, 'A thousand pardons, your excellency.' Then turning on his heel he walked from the room with his head thrown back in a proud and militant manner.

The incident stands out in my memory, for it was the only occasion during my stay in South Africa on which a colonial official favored a native in argument with an Englishman, and even in this case it was a

Dutchman who showed that courtesy and *he* was more than half drunk.

While we ate breakfast the attendants changed our mules. The fresh animals carried us forward at a great pace. We rode on hour after hour and at last came to Umtata on the borderline between the Transkei and Pondo Land. This town boasted not only a small college instituted by the missionaries, but also the seat of magistracy over the two adjoining countries. The official in charge was an old, white-haired, English general whose name I have forgotten. We had a long talk together while I was at Umtata and I gathered certain facts regarding the annexation of Pondo Land to Cape Colony. But in the typical English colonial manner he misinterpreted matters to suit his own ends.

After a short but pleasant stay we again took Cape-cart and after crossing the St. John's River started for the first time over Pondo soil. This country is as fertile and well watered as any in South Africa. All the impressions of the land I had gained while passing up and down the coast on the Pedro Gorino were more than confirmed. The exhilarating air, the green velvet meadows, the airy hills and distant mountains held me silent. In the willows and the blossoming mimosa trees that grew along the streams birds of a dozen varieties were singing. The game was even more plentiful than it had been in the Transkei and within the first two or three hours of our journey I noticed several types of antelope we had not seen before.

Emtinso and I shared the cart with two Englishmen. One was a magistrate, the other quite obviously a captain in Her Majesty's army. They were both over fifty, well fed, pompous and typical of their class. When the cart stopped in a little valley after fording a stream at one of the drifts, we all got down to stretch our legs. The officer addressed me patronizingly, 'How do you like our country?'

'Our country, indeed,' I thought. Yet I doubt if he caught my bitterness when I replied, 'It's good enough to hold any *body*.'

We arrived at Lusikisiki in the center of Pondo Land late in the afternoon. Emtinso took me to the home of one of his native friends, where we put up for the night.

CHAPTER XVII

SEGOW FAKU, KING OF THE PONDOS

THE next morning we prepared to leave for Kow Kenny, the kraal of Segow Faku. As there were no other means of conveyance we had to proceed afoot. We hired several native boys to carry our rather cumbersome luggage, and before the sun had risen we were on the trail. The winding path which we followed was so narrow that we had to walk single file. Often we met natives, and always they moved politely to one side to let us pass. We hurried forward as time was precious and my curiosity concerning the King of the Pondos was growing daily. As we journeyed our party became larger and larger. Natives joined us at every kraal. When it was learned that we were making a pilgrimage to Segow Faku the people along our way grew very respectful, and offered us food and huts in which to sleep.

In this sequestered region where fictitious reports would have one believe the most backward tribe in Africa resides we found the people cleanly, hospitable, and handsome. The huts in which they lived were far more sanitary than the 'negro' cabins of the Southern States, and furnished with soft karosses and simple furniture, they were quite as comfortable.

The first evening we stopped with one of the lesser chiefs, where we were treated royally. We were served a meal of broiled chicken, mushrooms cooked in ghee (a sort of native butter), wild tomatoes, umvoobu (a dish not unlike cottage cheese to which corn is added), and several varieties of fruit. All this was reënforced by a young kid beautifully baked which added the last touch to our feast. Who can say that such epicures are barbarians? Nor is good cooking confined to the southern part of the continent. The finest Irish stew I ever ate was at the geographical center of Africa, prepared by a native who did not know the world is round and had never heard of Ireland. But to return to our story.

One man at the hut of this chief said nothing but 'Umbala.' Every time the chief spoke this man uttered his single word until it grew to an enormous and terrible significance. It seemed like some dark incantation. At my first opportunity I asked Emtinso the meaning of the word. He said that it meant, 'It is true.' It seems that it was a rather general custom among the kings and chiefs to hire these hypnotic artists who continue to say, 'It is true, it is true,' until the natives believe every word their rulers tell them. In this case there was no harm done since the chief was of the better sort, but in many instances such devices employed by rascals work infinite harm.

It came to me at this time that the native Ethiopians' naïve confidence in their leaders might, if used to the right ends, prove their most valuable asset, but if abused as it has been in the past would surely keep them in an abased and lowly position. These people are like a confiding wife; they can see no error or defect, and that has been their downfall.

The next morning, after thanking the chief and his large family for their hospitality, we continued on our journey. We walked for several hours and at last on entering a broad and fertile plain we caught our first glimpse of Kow Kenny, kraal of King Segow Faku. We stopped at a distance to view the scene. The kraal was composed of some three or four hundred symmetrical huts clustered in an orderly arrangement about a central hut easily three or four times the size of any other. The kraal was situated in the midst of park-like country and shaded by fifty or more great trees. A stream passed through it and wound southward to join the St. John's River. As we approached we discerned several natives, the women in adequate native dress, with bright-colored handkerchiefs or cheetah-skin caps on their heads, the children more nearly naked. But by the time we entered the kraal every one had disappeared.

With Emtinso at the head of the column we advanced rapidly down a deserted path. At last we came to the huge hut we had seen from the plain; it was the dwelling-place of the King. Emtinso arranged us in a long line in front of this hut; then he said, 'Now take off hat, say, "changow." Bow and say "changow." '

We all bowed very low and simultaneously said the magic word. I learned later that 'changow' means the sun. Like a thousand other potentates the world over, Segow Faku wished to be identified with the most majestic symbol in the universe of our senses.

No one arrived, nothing happened. But Emtinso had fulfilled his duty and he now led us away to comfortable quarters. I was taken to the hut of one of his parishioners. The household consisted of a white-haired man of fifty, his younger wife, a girl of sixteen,

and two little boys. They were very shy, but hospitable. After Emtinso had introduced me to these
people he hurried away to see his own wife and family,
from whom he had been parted for many months.

After we had eaten, karosses were spread that I
might rest. It was scarcely past noon, yet the morning's walk through the hot sun had tired me to such an
extent that I was soon asleep. I was awakened at
three by Emtinso. His eyes were bright. He told me
to follow him quickly. The King had seen me as I
bowed before his hut and he was well pleased. He had
sent for me, and Emtinso did not wish to displease
him by keeping him waiting.

At first on entering the great hut from the sunlight
I was unable to distinguish anything. Then as my
eyes grew accustomed to the darkness I perceived such
a picture of majesty as one could not easily forget.
Twenty feet before me on a huge cowskin, squatted
like the Buddha, was Segow Faku, King of the Pondos.
His face was handsome, his skin shining black. His
body was enormous and beautifully muscled. He was
almost naked, his bright robe thrown to one side. He
wore only a breech-clout, a single necklace of teeth,
and a bracelet of ivory on one arm. An ostrich plume
adorned his hair.

At Emtinso's whisper we bowed low three times and
arose awaiting the King's pleasure. He held out his
hand, and when I took it in mine I realized what a
giant he was. The King spoke and Emtinso inter-
preted. He had said, 'Speak, friend.'

I told him briefly why I had come to Pondo Land
and thanked him for his courtesy. Emtinso again

served as interpreter. The King seemed pleased. He smiled, spoke a half-dozen guttural words, bowed his head three times and again shook my hand. It was evident that he liked me. After these formalities, I was introduced to the Fingo interpreter and the seventeen counselors grouped on each side of the King. I had scarcely noticed them before, I had been so fascinated by the potentate himself. Now there was more bowing and shaking of hands. At last a hundred or more prominent citizens were admitted to the hut. The covers were taken from three barrels of Kaffir beer and the drink flowed freely. After several hours, passed very pleasantly, we returned to our huts for the evening.

Early the next morning the King came to my door with a pure white chicken under his arm. He stood before my hut and called my name. I went out to meet him and accepted his present. He was some two inches taller than I and his splendid body shone in the sunlight. Having handed me the bird he spoke a few Pondo words and departed. It had all been as decorous as the bestowal of knighthood. Some months later, I shook hands with the Prince of Wales, now King of England, but it was with no such pride as I accepted a white cock from Segow Faku.

The natives who were my hosts were amazed at the honor. They had never seen the King come alone bearing the present of a white bird, and I was from that moment forth something superhuman in their eyes. In the days that followed, while I still tarried about the kraal, they treated me with a devotion that would have embarrassed me had I not been used to the ways of natives.

Every day or two I met the King. Often Emtinso was with me to translate our words. The King would ask me, 'Are you comfortable in your lodgings? Do you like our country? Will you live with us always?'

And I would reply, 'I am very comfortable, thank you. I think your country is the most fertile and beautiful in South Africa. I should like to stay here always, but I must return to my ship within a few weeks.'

I was very anxious to begin building schools and making arrangements for a mission. There were many problems to be solved and many difficulties to be overcome. But I knew it was best not to press matters. I saw the necessity of becoming fully acclimatized and fully acquainted with the country before venturing my entire plan. I knew that Segow Faku was as occupied with the thought of schools as I. But the ways of the native are not as direct and obvious as one might imagine. There is quite as much etiquette and decorum here as in any other part of the world. I realized that when the time was ripe the King would make the first move. I was merely awaiting a sign.

Meanwhile Emtinso had exhausted his exchequer. He decided that to support himself and his rather large family he would have to farm a piece of land and do his preaching in spare time. He came to me for money to buy stock and I gave him ten pounds. Very few people in Pondo Land have any money whatsoever. The ten pounds bought an enormous amount of material. Emtinso came home with a herd of cattle and goats, a flock of chickens, seeds of all kinds, and mealies and other food sufficient to feed a small army.

His prestige in the kraal was doubled and his sermons carried more weight than ever before.

I was not long awaiting a sign. I had been in Kow Kenny perhaps a week when the King came to my door one morning leading two fine horses. They were small as all Pondo horses are, but they were swift for their size and very spirited. Their coats had been brushed until they almost glittered. But joyful as I was at receiving these two splendid animals, I was even more joyful when on the same day the King informed me that he had made me one of his counselors. I knew that from that moment forth my advice would carry much weight.

CHAPTER XVIII

TWO STRANGE STORIES

IN the year 1782, the Grosvenor East Indiaman home-ward bound from Ceylon was wrecked off the south coast of Africa. She was reported to have had one million pounds sterling aboard, and silver coins are still picked up on the beach in the vicinity of the wreck. As in the case of hundreds of other ancient disasters, so many myths have sprung up surrounding it that it is hard to separate the truth from the fiction. Several of the accounts palpably false tell of terrible hardships endured by these people. Dozens of old romancers posing as historians have embellished the tale until it is generally believed that the survivors were forced to walk hundreds of miles through a burning desert-like country, subsisting almost entirely on carrion, being beaten, robbed and (in the case of the women) carried away by the natives, escaping the attacks of wild animals only by miracle, and, with the exception of a mere handful, dying before they reached the Cape.

As a matter of fact the ship was wrecked some twenty-five miles from what is now Port St. John's on the coast of Pondo Land, where the country was so fertile and the food so plentiful that a baby could have survived. As for the natives, knowing them as I do I have every reason to believe that they helped these unfortunate men and women.

I was at Kow Kenny over a century after the disaster when I learned of an old woman living some fifteen miles from the kraal who according to all reports had a skin almost as white as that of an English lady. A hundred stories centered about her. Some of the natives thought she was a goddess and had come on wings like a sea gull many years before. Some said that she was the daughter of the daughter of a castaway.

It came to my mind that she might be a descendant of one of the survivors from the Grosvenor. I was determined to look into the matter. With Emtinso to guide me I set forth one morning, and at last arrived at a neat stone house lying in a pleasant valley. A girl of perhaps fourteen met us at the door. Her skin was dark brown, but it seemed to me that there was a slightly Anglo-Saxon cast to her features. Emtinso spoke to her in Pondo, explaining something of the nature of our visit. She replied in the same musical tongue in which he had addressed her.

'What does she say, Emtinso?' I asked.

To my great surprise the girl herself answered and in English. 'I said that Grandmother is at home if you wish to see her,' she explained.

We were led into a bright little room, and there before an open window with the sunshine falling upon her sat the lady of whom we had heard. Rumor had not exaggerated the whiteness of her skin nor the Caucasian mold to her face. She was a woman of sixty-five or seventy, white-haired, proud in bearing, and soft spoken. As in the case of her granddaughter she used both English and Pondo.

I had not been mistaken in my surmise. This old

woman's mother's mother had been aboard the Grosvenor East Indiaman homeward bound from Ceylon
on that ill-fated trip. At our request she told the story
as it had come down by word of mouth. Occasionally
a quaint word like 'whilst' pointed to the fact that not
only the story but the use of the language as well had
been handed from mother to daughter. There was
remarkably little admixture of native or Boer words
and phrases. These people had, in a manner, lived to
themselves.

I had expected her story to be quite unlike the
written accounts of the wreck and in this I was not
disappointed. She spoke as if the castaways had actually liked the fertile shores upon which they had
been thrown, and while they had always dreamed of
some day returning to England they had settled in
Pondo Land rather than attempt the journey to the
Cape.

She seemed to delight in recounting the story, and
her words carried us back to the decks of the Grosvenor. Mary Cartwright was twenty-two that year,
and a widow of less than two months. She had accompanied her husband to India, for his regiment had
been detailed to foreign service shortly after their
marriage, and they could neither of them bear the
thought of parting. She had found the country so
unlike England that she had been homesick for
Devonshire, but the pleasure of being near her young
husband had outweighed all other considerations.

They had been married a little less than a year when
he was brought in one day sick with the fever. And
though she had nursed him day and night, he had at

last died, leaving her alone in a foreign country. Thus it was that she took passage on the Grosvenor East Indiaman and in 1782 was wrecked on the southeast coast of Africa. When the ship had gone aground the passengers had rushed to the deck in a panic. The surf was so high that all the attempts to launch lifeboats had been futile. A bold swimmer had at last carried a life-line to shore, and over this all but fifteen made their way to safety. Of those who perished on this first day, fourteen had fallen into the sea. The fifteenth was the cook who had been so drunk that he had refused to leave the ship.

Little had been salvaged. The small hoard of provisions was divided among the survivors, and they had set out toward the distant Cape unaware of their true position and of the difficulties they were about to encounter. They followed the coast, and were able to supplement their inadequate stores by gathering shellfish from the sea and picking fruits and berries, which they saw the birds eat freely, from the trees and bushes that grew on every hillside. At night they built great fires, more to keep up their courage than to protect them from wild animals, for they were in little danger on that score. During the day they carried lighted firebrands with them, for they had been able to salvage but one poor flint and steel from the wreck.

At first the women and children had been able to keep up. The men had assisted them wherever country was rough. At last, however, as they were increasingly aware of their distance from civilization, it was decided that all the sailors and most of the men would go on ahead and the women and children follow at their own pace. The hope was to reach help quickly and send a rescue-party to assist the women and children. After a sad leave-taking the men went forward, giving more of the provisions than they could easily spare to those who were to follow.

Two days later the women came to a river so wide and so deep that they were unable to cross it in any manner whatsoever. The men had either been able to swim it or had found native craft of some description to carry them across. The women were less fortunate and found the stream a perfect barrier against further progress.

The old woman paused a moment, smiled, and gazed out of the window. 'My grandmother,' she said, 'never heard the fate of those who went ahead. I have read stories of their journey which in many respects are to be doubted. It is said that on the sixth day after their parting with the women they ran out of provisions. They had come upon a region so dry and so barren that they could find no food wherewith to nourish their bodies, nor water wherewith they might quench their thirst. These accounts tell how they discovered thrown up upon the shore a dead seal, which they tore to pieces like wild beasts in their desire for food. It is stated that they walked weary miles with parched tongues, even drinking the sea water and worse. The mussels which they gathered here were so salt that they only increased their agony. Most doubtful of all are those parts of the stories which relate the brutality of the natives. My grandmother's story tells of nothing but kindness at the hands of the natives.

'But of the women who were left behind. . . .' She

pictured for us the crude camp these women made, waiting day after day for the rescue-party which never came. Mary Cartwright, alone with her thoughts, hardly cared what happened. Yet more than anything else she dreaded inactivity and the chance it gave her to brood. It was for this reason more than any other that she attempted the rash feat of swimming the mile of water at the river's mouth separating her from the far shore and consequently from the outer world. She had bid good-bye to her friends, put most of her clothing and her share of the provisions in a small pack tied upon her head, slipped into the water and struck out. For some time she had swum strongly, but before she had approached the other shore she was tiring rapidly. The slow current was carrying her toward the sea around a great bend in the river. At last when she looked back she could no longer see the women on the bank far behind her. Then just before exhaustion overtook her, a native canoe had slipped from the willows and a lithe black paddler had lifted her to safety.

The native was a young chief. He had come to fish in the estuary and had sat all afternoon among the willows catching catfish. He had caught all that he wanted and was preparing to make the trip back up the river to his kraal. Suddenly, to his great amazement, he had seen a very beautiful girl whose skin was apparently white, white as white mimosa blossoms, swimming feebly and being carried seaward. He had shot out with his canoe and lifted her into it.

She had gone with him to his kraal; nothing was of great importance now. She had liked the fertile country and the worship she received from the young chief and his natives. At last she had given him her body and her hand in native marriage. And she had not been unhappy in her long lifetime apart from her own people. Several times she had met others of the women who had survived the wreck. They all had native husbands, but their stories were not of violence. As lotus-eaters they forgot their native land and were happy here.

The woman before us smiled as if to say, 'There is little more to tell.' And then she asked us a little proudly, 'I am white, am I not, to come of a strain into which dark blood has been twice intermixed? I am really lighter than my mother.'

We assured her that she was as white as any English lady and I added, 'much more interesting.' She invited us to stay to dinner, but as we thought it necessary to return to Kow Kenny as soon as possible we declined with thanks. As we rode homeward, my mind was filled with the story of the wreck, and I wondered greatly that even in such an early day the natives were maligned to the outer world.

I was still dreaming of the Grosvenor when shortly after noon we reached Kow Kenny and were approached by a messenger from the King. The King wished us to come to his great hut, and Emtinso and I hurried forward. When we arrived he took us to a shaded mound some hundred feet from the doorway where we sat for a time talking of nothing in particular. Then the King asked, 'Have you heard the true story of how the Pondos lost their freedom?'

When Emtinso had translated, I assured Segow Faku I had not heard the story, whereupon he recounted an almost unbelievable tale of his recent trouble with the English Colonial officials. He recounted how Cecil Rhodes, Prime Minister of Cape Colony, usurped his power and stole from him his hereditary jurisdiction over Pondo Land. Here is the story as he told it to me:

Some five or six years before, six Cape-carts had come to Pondo Land, carrying altogether thirty or thirty-five Europeans garbed as missionaries. These people were given a hospitable welcome by the un-sophisticated natives. They were given food to eat and huts in which to sleep. They had accepted the natives' hospitality and for several weeks had surveyed and observed the country. Then one day they left as suddenly and as mysteriously as they had come. They arrived at Lusikisiki and by a preconceived plan wired Cecil Rhodes that the Pondos were rising. There was great excitement throughout Cape Colony. Rhodes had immediately ordered British regiments to occupy Pondo Land. They had come in three great columns, from the north and from the west and from the south. They had entered this peaceful country shooting at everybody they saw. Any little group of natives huddled together in fear was a sufficient excuse for a charge. Scores of innocent Pondos were butchered.

There was not a single case of resistance, for these people were not only entirely unarmed, but they were attacked without warning and without provocation. The occupation by the British regiments was a complete surprise. When the advance guard reached Kow Kenny and threw their guns in Segow Faku's face there was not a more astonished man in Africa. The report that the Pondos had risen was absolutely false. They had had nothing to rise against, having been independent until this time, and they had no effective arms with which to rise; the English had seen to that. They were merely a peace-loving, pastoral people without malice, less savage by far than the land-mad Englishmen who had poured down upon them.

Segow Faku together with his counselors was arrested and taken to Cape Town. All during the months of his absence the regiments were billeted upon the impoverished natives. The King had to sustain an expensive trial in Cape Town. When at last he was acquitted of all charges brought against him he returned to his once prosperous and happy country only to find it a shadow of its former self. Ninety thousand of the hundred thousand head of cattle had been confiscated. The country was subjected to a killing taxation designed to keep it from ever again reaching a powerful state. Thus the Pondos overnight were reduced from opulence to poverty.

'There,' said the King, pointing to nine obsolete rifles leaning against his hut, 'is the entire armament of a once powerful nation.' Then his eyes became suddenly fierce and the great muscles of his body quivered; his voice became hoarse with passion. 'Sé-si-boń-wa-ngá-bezi-zwe-ná. (Even now the white man watches us.)' Then Emtinso, raised to a high pitch of excitement by the story, shouted, 'Lí-zo-dú-me-li-mutá-te. (We shall strike them and take them prisoners.)'

What could I do? I wished to quiet these men, show them that only through development of mind could they rise above the invaders. But I myself was overwhelmed with anger, and I could not use cold logic and impersonal arguments on a subject that stirred my emotions as this one did.

That evening I wrote this note to a friend back in the United States:

DEAR ALFRED:

To-day I have heard two strange stories. The first was the story of the wreck of the Grosvenor from the lips of a descendant of one of the survivors. It would merely entertain you. The second was such a tale of imperialism as has never before come to my ears. I am sure it would anger you through and through.

I have never been able to conceive the imperialists as anything but vulgar murderers and thieves, whose egotistical, crafty and cunning natures hold no respect for intellectual or moral values, but upon hearing the story of the unlawful annexation of Pondo Land to Cape Colony as it has just been related by Segow Faku, King of the Pondos, my estimation of their nature puts them upon even a lower level than heretofore.

Nothing will deter these men save physical power superior to their own and sufficiently strong to strike terror into their leathern hearts. Their principal activity is marching up and down the world sowing dragon's teeth, and their principal aim to amass more gold than any who went before them.

Unless humanity learns to choose for its leaders philosophers instead of the megalomaniacs they have been choosing for the past sixteen centuries, their mechanical inventions and arms of precision will eventually help them to destroy themselves and to wipe the human race from the face of the earth.

Your friend,
(*Capt.*) HARRY DEAN

CHAPTER XIX

THE END OF AN OLD FEUD

ALMOST every day there were more talks with the King. I explained the strategic position of his country, its resources and possibilities. I discussed the future of Port St. John's and, as an old seaman, offered my advice as to improvements in the little harbor. I extolled the civilizing effects of religion, for although I was not religious myself I was in favor of establishing a mission for the natives. Most of my arguments, however, were on the subject of education, and I made him understand that if the Pondos were ever to be a great people they would have to be given instruction in the rudiments with opportunity for higher education. Above all, I extolled nautical science and the discipline of the sea.

The King was more than willing to help me, and told me of a valley twenty miles from Kow Kenny where I might have all the land I wished for building schools.

Early one morning we saddled our horses and started out to see the valley and the site for the proposed schools. After a two-hours' ride we entered a rocky ravine, along which our horses were forced to move single file. We went downward toward a river whose blue-green surface showed now and again through the vines and foliage. When we at last reached the river's brink I was aware of a noise like that of distant thunder. I asked Emtinso the source of the sound and he explained that we were approaching the Tsitza waterfall, which is the highest in Cape Colony. We followed a narrow, beaten path along the river bank through a gorge bright with flowers. The current rushed along ahead of us and became swifter and swifter as we advanced. At last, upon rounding a bend, we found ourselves at the crest of the fall. I have seen Niagara, Yosemite, the falls of the Zambezi, and many more, but none that were as beautiful as this.

The river at this point was of a good size, and its waters fell in a sheer, unbroken drop of three hundred and seventy-five feet, thundering onto the rocks below and dancing high into the clear air. The valley beneath us stretched away for many miles, with the river winding through it like a silver ribbon. The floor of the valley was a green meadow, the hills enclosing it were clothed with forests.

It made us excited and heady to look over the jagged cliff at the dancing water below. Our horses moved nervously on the narrow, rocky promontory overlooking the fall, and watched the river with frightened eyes. But Segow Faku rode his fine black mare to within a few inches of the rim and sat as proudly as a feudal baron viewing his domain. It was as if this man and horse were unmoved by the petty emotions and fears of the lesser individuals of their respective species.

We took a path that went around the cliff and by easy descent came to the valley floor. It must have taken us several miles to descend the three hundred and seventy-five feet that the water took at one bound. When we were at last below, looking upward, the sound of falling water was almost deafening. Some hundred feet from the fall itself the foaming, turbulent stream subsided into a quiet pool of great depth, where bright fish of every size darted. As several of the boys were armed with spears it was suggested that we rest for a few hours and fish. We fished and speared half the morning, catching all that we wanted for the kraal.

Then we stripped and swam, sporting in the cool water and diving downward toward the bottom, where the greater fish lurked in the shadows.

Below the pool, the river ran away in a rapid stream some sixty or seventy feet wide following the valley toward the sea. When we had dressed, we mounted, and rode down along its banks toward the point the King had chosen for the building of schools and a mission. As I turned and looked back, the waterfall and the cliff curving away on either side seemed back-drops to a magnificent stage, a stage fit for any drama man might conceive. And I wondered if that drama were not about to be enacted. Could the stage setting be too stupendous that was to form the background for the rehabilitation of Africa and the foundation of an Ethiopian Empire? What cities might spring up in this valley; what temples flower like mimosa bloom?

When we had ridden three or four miles the sound of the waterfall was again like distant thunder, very drowsy and soothing. At last the King turned his horse from the river and told us to follow him. We ascended a gradual slope until we had risen some forty feet and were four hundred feet from the river bank. 'This is yours,' he said, and with a sweep of his hand indicated a large level meadow high enough to be dry even in the rainy season, and broad enough to accommodate scores of buildings. I thanked him from the bottom of my heart, realizing that very soon my schools would stand where now we saw nothing but grass billowing in the wind. We returned to Kow Kenny, where papers were signed by the King and his counselors giving the African Methodist Church one thousand four hundred morgens of land for the purpose of building schools and a mission.

The very next day I went to the under-chief, who controlled the valley, and arranged for materials and labor. I decided to live with an English trader and his mulatto wife, who owned a small station within two miles of my concession. They took me willingly. The chief and his men worked industriously gathering material, and within two weeks three buildings were under way. I had drawn the plans for them myself and they were quite unlike any architecture in South Africa. The floors and the lower walls were of a good grade of stone which we quarried from one of the cliffs near the waterfall. The upper walls, which were very well protected by the wide eaves, were of adobe brick, which I taught the natives to make from the fine clay of the valley. The timbers were hand-hewn from the near-by forest.

I had just become thoroughly absorbed in my work when I was summoned to Kow Kenny by a messenger who galloped up to me on a foam-flecked horse. I mounted and followed him to the Knig's kraal as fast as I could ride. Long before we got there we could hear drums beating, and from every corner of the horizon see the warriors gathering. When we reached the kraal I dismounted and hurried to the King's hut. The counselors were assembled and the King was very grave. I found that war with the Pondo Mesis was almost inevitable.

There are only two things which are of sufficient importance to cause the natives to go to war; one is their land, the other their women. Several of the Pondo Mesi boys from the tribe northwest of Pondo Land had eloped with Pondo girls and carried them away to their mountainous country. In the native code of morals this is a heinous crime, and may only be avenged with blood. Practically all the counselors were in favor of immediate attack, and the fever for battle was rampant in the kraal. Even as we talked the army was forming into the typical formation, its battle-line arranged in the shape of a bull's horns, with the men facing the enemies' country. Even as we talked the warriors were swinging their assegais, dancing the war dance, and working themselves to a tremendous emotional pitch.

I saw that it would be a superhuman feat to cool the anger of these thousands of people, but I was determined to try. I asked for a chance to speak and the King granted me the privilege. Emtinso stood by my side and translated rapidly into Pondo. I said: 'The Pondo Mesis have done you a great wrong and you must be avenged. They have stolen your girls and carried them up into the mountains. You know but one answer to such an insult, war! You will attack and there will be a great battle. Men will be killed and huts will be burned, but this should not deter brave warriors. You will advance with assegais in hand and descend upon the Pondo Mesis. In your absence the mealies will rot in the fields and your unwatched herds will wander into other countries. But that is nothing when you think of the glory of victory. You will fight a great fight. Many women will be widowed. You will continue to do battle until every warrior in one of the armies is dead or captured, or until the Pondo or the Pondo Mesi King lies dead. Then the women of the unfortunate tribe who lost in battle will spend their lives in a foreign land under a foreign king. These are small sacrifices, however, when you dream of vengeance. Your law is your law and I will not try to dissuade you. But wait! What is it you would avenge? Intermarriage between two tribes? Are you so sure the Pondo Mesis are another tribe? Some of your old men can remember when the two tribes were one. They can remember when there was no feud. They can remember when these men whom you are about to kill sat beside you at the feasts and aided you in battle against your common enemies. The same blood that runs in your veins runs in theirs. These boys and girls would merely reunite two tribes that should be one. Still if you must have vengeance. . . .'

Those people were by no means invulnerable to logic, and one by one the counselors were convinced that war should be averted.

By a lucky coincidence an embassy of Pondo Mesis arrived while I was still talking. Segow Faku, having gained implicit confidence in my ability, placed in my hands the great trust of coming to terms and avoiding war. I addressed them before Segow Faku and his counselors and tried to show them the great necessity of coming to terms. The palaver lasted all that day and the next. Finally I said, 'We have talked long enough. King Segow Faku will keep peace under these conditions: You must send the young men together with their stolen wives back to Pondo Land where they will work for their fathers-in-law and become Pondos, dropping their former tribal affiliations. You must bring labola of one hundred head of cattle and one hundred head of goats to pacify Segow Faku and his people. That this old feud may die, you must agree never again to insult or fight with the Pondos. If you will not submit to these terms we will advance with our army and wipe you off the face of the earth.'

The Pondo Mesis gathered together and talked and argued. One great warrior was all for fighting. Every few minutes he would wave his arms and howl defiance at all things Pondo. However, the older men of the embassy realized that our terms were very liberal and that it would be wise to accept. That evening they came to Segow Faku and promised to comply with all his terms if their King found them suitable. The next morning they mounted and left for their own country.

I stayed at Kow Kenny for a week to make sure that all the warriors departed. By the end of the week the Pondo Mesi boys and their wives arrived, driving before them the herd of cattle and goats. Thus an old feud which had smoldered for years, and had on several occasions burst into angry flame, came to an end. War had been averted by a miracle, and a firm foundation for friendship laid where only hatred had existed before.

The next morning I returned to my schools and recommenced work upon the buildings in earnest. I had been working several hours when I became the victim of a most peculiar attack. Great packs of Scotch collies who have gone wild, roam this country like wolves, pulling down whatever game they come upon. I had left the laborers and had walked to the far side of one of the buildings when I saw one of these packs rushing down upon me. I was alone and unarmed. It was a moment for fast thinking. By great good fortune a big hoe that had been used in mixing clay was leaning against the building. This I grasped and held before me awaiting the attack. The leader bounded into the hoe with such violence that he fell back unconscious. The rest closed in snapping and snarling. I backed myself against the building and swung left and right but the dogs still came on, springing for my throat. I continued to fight them off, but where one dog fell another took his place. In a moment the natives heard the uproar and hurried to my assistance. They beat off the infuriated animals with their knobkerries, but not before one of the dogs had ripped an ounce of flesh from the calf of my right leg.

CHAPTER XX

WE HUNT A MAN-EATING LION

Some days later I was again called to Kow Kenny. A Pondo Mesi messenger had just arrived, begging aid from the Pondos. His people would never have asked their neighbors for help had it not been that the differences between the two tribes had just been adjusted. The occasion of the plea was a lion hunt. A wicked old man-eater had been coming down out of the Stormberg Mountains for years to kill the Pondo Mesi children and carry them away. On a number of occasions attempts had been made to capture him, but the crafty old rascal had always made his escape to his almost impenetrable mountain retreat. In his last attack he had killed the chief's favorite child. The tribe was determined to capture the lion at any cost.

Segow Faku had sent for me to aid in the hunt, promising that work would go forward on the buildings during my absence. He realized that the only honorable thing we could do, considering the recent truce, was to help the weaker tribe. Much to the messenger's joy the King sent eighteen men on horseback and five of his nine guns. Emtinso, who was a good hunter, was given full charge of the expedition.

I was glad to comply with the King's wish and accompany the hunters, as the past three weeks had been strenuous and I stood in need of diversion. I took with me an English army rifle, a shotgun, and revolvers which I had brought from the Pedro Gorino.

We equipped ourselves for a ten-days' journey, and when all was ready mounted our horses and set forth. For many hours we rode through a garden-like country dotted with small clumps of trees. It was sunny weather and not a cloud in the sky. About the middle of the afternoon Emtinso shot a buck which had started up before us and one of the native boys slung the carcass up behind him on his horse. By night we had come to the St. John's River and here we made our camp.

At this point the river was fordable, the horses being able to wade, except in mid-channel, where they were forced to swim for a few yards. Farther down the river nearer the coast it became a slow, meandering stream with heavy sub-tropical vegetation on either side. Farther above us it was rapid, swift, and treacherous.

From our camp we could see the massive, rugged country about the Stormberg Mountains.

For our evening meal we had mealies. If we had been at home in Kow Kenny we should have added beef, or chicken, or goat's meat to the half-sack of corn. Instead we dressed the buck and the birds we had shot during the day and cooked them with the grain in a great iron pot.

The next day brought us higher into the foothills. We were following the middle branch of the St. John's River, and we rode for miles along the bank of the rushing stream. Sometimes it fell in waterfalls or tumbled in rapids down its rocky channel. Sometimes it moved more slowly through deep pools cut in the rocks. We were some three thousand feet above sea level at this time, and the air was clear and bracing.

The country was barren and dry, cut with gulches

and gulleys. We had to take care in places that the horses did not fall. I was particularly careful of my little mare, as she had been given to me by the King and I was very fond of her. In the afternoon of the second day we came into a little fertile valley, and there lay the kraal of the King of the Pondo Mesis.

These people had just enough contact with the outside world to respect church affiliations and European clothes. With either of these distinctions your social rating was beyond question. Some of the natives had red handkerchiefs, some shirts, some shoes or a necktie. The King had an almost complete outfit, and he strutted about proudly in his regalia. The more subtle indications of culture were lost on these people, but its outward manifestations affected them mightily.

I was a messenger from King Segow Faku and Emtinso was a preacher in the African Methodist Episcopal Church, so we were accorded a royal welcome. We were given the best house in the kraal and feasted from morning to night. Our hut like the others was the shape of a beehive, built of wattles, mud, and sticks with a grass roof. It had windows and was some thirty feet in diameter. The floor was packed hard and was almost as artistic as a floor of mosaic, as designs of a dozen varieties, complicated and perfect in their execution, had been wrought upon its surface. It was easy to see from these phantastic conceptions that the people were not only good craftsmen, but very imaginative as well.

When we were presented to the King, he made a long speech. He thanked us for our willingness to help him in his hour of need. And he proceeded to explain what a benefit we were about to bestow upon his people. He told us that in the heart of this old lion lived the spirit of Gafu, a rival chief. When this chief was angry, he stirred the old rascal lion from within and made him steal the Pondo Mesi children. He told us that if we killed the lion, Gafu would die also and there would be no more war or trouble with his tribe. The King had never before mentioned this to his people and when he finished speaking there was great excitement and much discussion. Most of the natives agreed that the King's theory explained nicely the perversion of the old beast. It put a new importance on the outcome of the hunt.

For two days we stayed about the kraal, learning the history of the man-eater and all his habits. We were told how and where he made his kills, how often he came down out of the mountains, and in what direction he retreated. The land over which we were about to travel was too rough for the horses, so when we felt we were ready we gathered together our forces, picked out the best dogs in the camp and proceeded on foot. Seven of us were armed with guns. I had my two revolvers and a rifle. A son of the chief of the Pondo Mesis carried my shotgun. Emtinso and his four best Pondo boys carried Segow Faku's five rifles. And the other thirty-five natives were armed with sticks, assegais, knobkerries, and knives.

We set forth early one morning and soon came to the place where the chief's son had been killed. A small volcanic mound of black sand, a regular diamond prospect, still showed the marks of the struggle. The child had been carrying water from the watering-place a half mile beyond and on his return had stopped to play in the fine sand. The lion lying in wait in a clump of brush near the trail had taken the child from the rear. There were still a few pieces of blood-stained clothing scattered about. We put the dogs' noses to these and the ground about them. Suddenly one wandering from the others picked up the scent, then the whole pack, baying and howling, shot off across the barren country in the direction of the Stormberg Mountains. We followed at a trot, calling in the dogs whenever they got too far in advance. As we were crossing a karroo cut with ravines and dry water-courses we found it rough going.

Only once during the afternoon did the dogs lose the scent. Their confusion gave us a much-needed chance to rest and a half-hour for shooting lesser game. I shot several birds and one of the boys got a blesbok. At last the trail was rediscovered and we again hurried forward.

When night overtook us we were in a ravine through which a trickle of water ran. The tiny stream appeared and disappeared into the gravel again, as do so many creeks in this part of the country. We had gone up the gully several hundred yards when we came upon unmistakable indications that the lion had recently passed this way. And since it was dark and we were sure that we were on the right trail we soon decided on a likely spot and made our camp. Cutting some dead wood from the mimosa growth along the water-course we started a fire, and having dressed and washed our blesbok, doves, and grouse started them cooking. After we had eaten, we built other fires in a circle about us to keep the snakes away. The rapid pace over the rough country had tired us all and we were soon asleep.

When a lion gets so old that he can no longer take great springs, landing among herds of buck and killing them left and right with his terrible blows and slashes, he will sometimes take to eating human flesh. Often these man-eaters are very unkempt, ragged-looking old brutes, but they seem to have learned new lessons in strategy from their contact with human beings, and they are very hard to capture and kill.

We realized the crafty nature of our prey and the next morning we proceeded more carefully. We unleashed the dogs and set them on the trail again, but we did not let them run so far ahead and we watched each bush and hiding-place more closely than before. The scent was stronger here and the dogs followed the trail with no trouble at all. I saw to my rifle and revolvers, determined to get a shot if one offered.

At noon we came to a water-hole and surprised two buck which we shot for dinner. The natives had reached such a pitch of excitement about the old lion that they talked and laughed incessantly. They would scarcely stop to rest or eat despite the fatiguing morning, but wished to be on the trail again following the dogs.

We were well up in the mountains now, and early in the afternoon the country through which we were traveling became so rugged that we were forced to go single file. Emtinso, whom we all acknowledged as the best shot, went first, I came second, and the rest of the boys filed along behind. About three o'clock in the afternoon the dogs led us into a rocky gorge with sheer walls rising on either side. A clear stream trickled over the uneven floor and part of the time we were forced to wade up this stream because of the narrowness of the canyon.

Suddenly we heard the dogs go crazy up ahead. We hurried around a sharp bend and found ourselves in a little natural amphitheater with high rocky walls and no possible entrance except the pass in which we now stood. Emtinso, who had entered a few seconds before, had shouted, 'There he is.' By the time I reached his side, however, there was no lion in sight, only three of our dogs ripped wide open and groveling and howling near a clump of bushes on the far side of the enclosure. The rest of the pack were cowering back and trembling like leaves. No one but Emtinso had seen the man-eater, but there was no doubt that we had him cornered. We decided that this must be his home and the place he had been hiding these many years while he preyed upon the Pondo Mesis.

We could have rushed the bush and killed him, but we decided on a safer and surer course. Climbing up the steep walls of the amphitheater to the plateau surrounding it, we stationed our men every twenty feet with the seven guns equidistant, and hid ourselves over the edge to wait.

About sunset we were rewarded. The old monarch crept forth, cautiously at first, then very boldly. He yawned, stretched, and made his way down to the stream to drink. We waited until he had his fill, and then as he started back for the bush Emtinso gave us the sign and we let him have it with all seven guns. With one contortive spring the lion threw himself high into the air, then fell to the ground trembling and lay still. When we skinned him, we found a bullet from my forty-five rifle just behind his shoulder, almost over his heart. So I had killed him and the skin was given to me.

The natives were so happy they were almost crazy. They danced and shouted, laughed and sang, all the while the lion was being skinned. They heaped abuses on the dead carcass, and added insult to injury by recounting over and over how neatly we had trapped the old rascal and how ridiculous he looked now he had lost his skin. Vengeance was sweet to these simple people.

We camped in the amphitheater that night and the next morning before daybreak started back toward the home kraal. It had taken us two days to get to the lion, but by taking short cuts that the natives knew we were able to return to the Pondo Mesis in less than a day. Towards noon we ran across a large herd of wild ostriches. We could not stop to capture them, but I had one of the natives promise to keep track of their movements.

When we arrived at the Pondo Mesi kraal we entered in a sort of triumphal march carrying the skin proudly. The good news spread quickly and soon natives were pouring in from every point of the compass. Then the celebration began. Because of the superstition that the spirit of Gafu was in the lion, these people expected word every hour that their enemy's chief was dead.

The celebration was a combination of a barbecue and a revival meeting. The King had goats and cattle and sheep and chickens killed. These were dressed and rolled in clay and laid in a pit full of hot stones. When the meat was thoroughly roasted, the shell of clay was cracked off, and the quarters of beef, legs of lamb, and roast birds were piled high before the King, who sat on a nicely tanned cowhide and served his guests.

Each of the three or four thousand natives attending the festival was given a new fiber mat from which to eat and the public love-feast began. The King did not eat; he was host.

In return for the King's hospitality every one gave him presents.

Then the dancing began. There were dances of every kind, many of them improvised. The most important event of the evening was a magnificent war-dance. The natives sang in weird harmony and played their three-stringed guitars far into the night. There was a bright moon and its light and the light of the fires threw giant shadows from the dancers. The great warrior who had proved obstreperous at Kow Kenny led the war-dance. He stood almost a head above his fellows, and they themselves were big men. When the dance was over and the others had thrown themselves exhausted to the ground he seemed as fresh as ever. For a moment he stood alone in the circle of faces, the firelight gleaming upon him. Then he struck up a dance of his own. Throwing himself fiercely about, leaping high into the air, swinging his assegai around and around his head, and making low guttural noises, he retreated and advanced before the King. Emtinso and I who were sitting one on each side of the King were the guests of honor, for we had killed the lion. This was what made the great warrior jealous. As Emtinso explained, this enormous native was telling the King all the things he had done in battle, and the King was bowing in acknowledgment. The warrior wanted to impress upon the King that killing a lion was nothing; he could kill lions bare-handed. He was saying, 'It isn't right to make peace with these Pondos. Next time you want lions killed send for me. I'm a great warrior.' The King was a diplomat; therefore he bowed and smiled, bowed and smiled.

The natives drank great quantities of Kaffir beer and ate and ate. They were still celebrating when we went to bed at dawn.

CHAPTER XXI

A CHAPTER ON DEATH

BEFORE we left, the King of the Pondo Mesis gave Emtinso and me presents of skins and carved ivory. He also entrusted us with several fine horses, which he wished us to present to Segow Faku on our return to Kow Kenny. He was so grateful for the aid the Pondos had given him in killing the lion, and for the very liberal terms he had received at the hands of the Pondo King, that he had decided to swear allegiance to Segow Faku, thus joining the two tribes under the one leader. On our return to Kow Kenny we carried news of the successful hunt and of the forthcoming coalition of the two tribes. Segow Faku was greatly pleased, as were all his subjects. The good news spread rapidly and soon all Pondo Land was celebrating and feasting. The natives awaited with excitement the arrival of the King of the Pondo Mesis.

My joy was short-lived. I had been at Kow Kenny less than a week when a messenger arrived from Port St. John's carrying this letter:

CAPTAIN DEAN:

The Pedro Gorino is at anchor here in the harbor. Captain Peter Benjamin lies aboard her sick with the fever. Our trip has been one of misfortune. Although we had some luck in our whaling in the Mozambique Channel, on our return we ran into a bad squall near Cape St. Andrew. A southeaster hit us square on the port before we could reef and we lost the new sails with which you rigged her. We are using the old ones again and they are in pretty bad shape. Then just out of Delagoa Bay we were overhauled by a British man-of-war and were made to show our papers. This with other delays and annoyances at the hands of the British has eaten up much of the profits. Now Captain Benjamin is raving with fever. Please come at once.

Respectfully,
WILL BRAITHWAITH
Officer in Command

I saw that it would be necessary to go to Port St. John's and perhaps sail the Pedro Gorino into Cape Town. I told the King and his counselors just how matters stood, and they agreed that there was no other course. Before leaving, I had Segow Faku and Emtinso promise that, should I never return, the mission and schools would be completed just as if I were there. The King, however, clung to the hope that I could return before the next rainy season. He was so sad that at first I thought of taking him with me. It was forgetful of me even to think of it. I had forgotten that since the annexation of Pondo Land to Cape Colony his status was virtually that of a prisoner-of-war. His every move was watched with suspicion, and should I have taken him on a journey to Cape Town it would have endangered his country and given the English an excuse for new atrocities.

I hurriedly gathered together my luggage, and with Emtinso, Segow Faku's nine-year-old son, and several natives for companions on the first leg of my journey, mounted and galloped away toward Port St. John's. When we reached the St. John's River we followed its valley, which cuts deeper and deeper as it approaches the sea. By the time we reached the harbor we were between hills which rise over a thousand feet on each side of the river. The country here was clothed with dense subtropical vegetation of a deep glossy green broken now and again with the brighter colors of birds and flowers.

When I saw the Pedro Gorino lying at anchor I was anxious to go aboard and once more feel the deck beneath my feet. I signaled for a boat and was soon being rowed across the waters of the harbor. Even before we reached her side I could see that the ship had seen rough weather. This and the fact that my good friend Peter Benjamin was sick with the fever filled me with despondency. Braithwaith hailed me across the water, but when I had clambered aboard we scarcely hesitated long enough to greet each other. Instead we hurried to the cabin to see Peter Benjamin. He was delirious and he did not recognize me. He rolled and tumbled in his berth crying, 'Ahoy, ahoy,' or 'Sally a drink, a drink, girl.' Again he would sing bits of a chanty or groan most pitifully.

'Has he had any attention?' I asked.

Braithwaith seemed a little hurt as he assured me that Benjamin had been given quinine and all the other simple remedies for fever, together with every care. I could see that there was only one chance for his recovery and that was a quick run for Cape Town. I went ashore, carrying with me all the suitable presents I could find in the cargo aboard the boat. These I presented to Emtinso and my native friends. I then wrote a farewell letter to the King, telling him that I had not forgotten his kindness nor the beauty of his country and promising some day to return to Kow

Kenny. Segow's little son, who had ridden all the way with the ability of a mature horseman, broke down and cried when he learned that I was really leaving. Great tears rolled down his shiny, black face and he was only to be consoled by the largest stick of candy I could purchase in Port St. John's.

Because of the extreme necessity of reaching Cape Town we put to sea that evening and bowled along under full sail. The night was clear, and as we sailed Will Braithwaith told me the story of the ship's voyaging since I had last been aboard. At every port the officials had delayed the papers. The cargoes from De Costa at Delagoa Bay and from Freighter and Elliott at Cape Town had been decreasing steadily. The storm which had taken the new set of sails had also washed away a considerable amount of whaling gear, and damaged the superstructure we had built in the waist. Not the least depressing was Will Braithwaith's deep and mournful voice. There was a feeling about the ship hard to define, a feeling of foreboding. It came over me like a spell. I wished to shake myself free. Although the weather was warm, the white moonlight on the deck seemed as cold as winter in the mountains. The wind went sighing through the rigging like the voices of departing spirits.

Before the night had passed, the sky had clouded over. Day after day the world grew darker. Each man in the crew felt death hanging over the ship and never passed the cabin except in fear. What evil spirits might be lurking about us? They rolled their big eyes. As if they could smell death, the sharks followed us day and night. Gulls uttering hoarse cries stormed about us.

Peter Benjamin grew continually worse. In spite of all we could do he raved and lost consciousness. I attended him many hours each day and often sat up with him through the long watches of the night. Once in a rational moment he asked to be buried on an island where he could hear the swishing of the waves on the shore. He had been born on an island and he loved the sea. He told me bits of his childhood and his early life aboard ship. Then he lost consciousness again and began singing broken bits of song. Often I could not understand the words or make out the tune. Then, as if he had found one with more meaning than the rest, his voice cleared to its customary deep, bell-like tone and he burst forth singing the chanty sailors sing at landfall when the journey is almost over:

> 'Only one more day a-reefin'
> One more day,
> Oh rock and roll me over
> Only one more day.'

Peter Benjamin knew as well as we that he was about to die. I hoped for his sake that it might happen before he reached Cape Town, so that he might be buried at sea or upon an island as he had wished. But as we drew nearer and nearer Cape Town we saw that he might last until we got him ashore, and we hoped against hope that some great doctor might save him. Upon dropping anchor in Table Bay we hurried him to a hospital, where the diagnosis was blackwater fever and a weak heart.

I came to see him every day, but it was evident that he was growing weaker. On the third morning I asked the doctor what chances he had, if any. He replied callously, 'There's no use fooling with a patient with a heart like that. He's been dying for twenty years.' The next day we received word that Benjamin was dead.

We arranged for a fine funeral. Every man aboard the ship bought a top hat, a Prince Albert coat, and black crêpe for mourning. It was attended by the crew and a great many Africando and European friends, including the old Scotchmen, Mr. Freighter and Mr. Elliott. Altogether there must have been one hundred and seventy-five of us marching behind the hearse. He was buried from Will Braithwaith's house and after the ceremony we marched the whole length of Hanover Street and out to the cemetery. Since he was an African his death was soon forgotten, except by his friends aboard the ship. . . .

A year later another funeral in Cape Town attracted world-wide notice because it was for a conqueror of Africa instead of one of her sons. Cecil Rhodes, grandiose and pompous in life, could scarcely have been expected to be simple and unassuming in death.

Until his physicians had insisted upon a change of climate, he had remained at his estate, the magnificent Groote Schuur. Then he had been borne to the sea-shore where it was hoped that the lower altitude might aid his heart. But money was unavailing at the last, and he died, proving himself no more immortal than the thousands of poor natives who had died at his hands. What did it avail him that he had been able to trick an old chief out of an Aladdin's cave full of diamonds, gold, and rare skins in return for a few hundred guns which would not shoot? What did all his confiscations and annexations, his wide estates and unlimited wealth avail him? It is said that his brother killed himself in Central Africa by getting drunk during an attack of the fever, which so befuddled his poor brain that he poured a keg of alcohol over himself and lit a match. Cecil Rhodes was no less a victim of his vices.

He was an imperialist to the last, and at his own suggestion his burial was the very symbol of imperialism. He was drawn up Adderley Street on a gun carriage drawn by black horses and draped with flags. A retinue of thousands followed him to his grave in the Matopa Hills up in Matabeleland. Here, by an order he had given before his death, he was placed in a great cement crypt weighing thousands of pounds, poured into a cave blasted from the solid granite. Thus his body might never be removed from the country he had conquered, and his iron spirit might continue to subdue the Ethiopian race even after he was gone. This was the last grandiose gesture of an African conqueror whose cruelty was only equaled by that of Henry the Navigator.

Yet six months afterwards (since Africa is a warm country), he was no more in the eyes of nature than Peter Benjamin, remembered only by his shipmates.

BOOK IV
THE NET DRAWS TIGHTER

CHAPTER XXII

THE QUEEN OF THE BASUTOS

No, no, go not to Lethe, neither twist
  Wolf's-bane, tight-rooted, for its poisonous wine;
Nor suffer thy pale forehead to be kiss'd
  By nightshade, ruby grape of Proserpine;
Make not your rosary of yew-berries,
  Nor let the beetle, nor the death-moth be
    Your mournful Psyche, nor the downy owl
A partner in your sorrow's mysteries;
  For shade to shade will come too drowsily,
    And drown the wakeful anguish of the soul.

KEATS

As the train rolled on toward Bloemfontein I told myself that all was not well. As Will Braithwaith had intimated, the officials were attempting to undermine my business, but this worried me less than an indiscretion of my own.

I had found among many enemies one who seemed to be a new friend. William Price, a young Englishman, had gained the implicit confidence of Benjamin before that good sailor's death. While Freighter and Elliott's cargoes had been falling off, Price had been securing contracts for the Pedro Gorino from other sources. At last he had been handling so much of the shore business at Cape Town that he had become virtually the ship's agent. On my recent visit to Cape Town I had met Price for the first time and had taken a liking to him from the start. His eyes had seemed a trifle narrow, though gray and frank, and his countenance had appeared to me to be open and friendly.

Yet, as the wheels of the train clicked monotonously on the rails and as I left Cape Town farther and farther behind, I told myself I had been duped.

Why had Price insisted that I transfer my money to the bank in which he held stock? 'Easier to arrange for credit,' he had said. It had seemed plausible at the time, but it seemed insufficient reason now.

And why had I become so garrulous with Price and with the bank's officials? Their courtesy was not founded on friendship, it was merely my deposit of several thousand pounds — sufficient reason for civility anywhere in the world. Of course I had realized that in the near future I was going to need a loan of a considerable amount of money, but I should not have run the risk of putting my entire plan before these people.

It had all come about quite naturally. Lerothodi, King of Basutoland, and the most powerful ruling native in South Africa, had heard of my desire to help the Ethiopian race. He and his favorite wife, Queen Baring, were anxious to secure my help and had invited me to visit them in their fertile and mountainous country. They had practically promised me a sizable concession of land in return for my services and I had been anxious to accept their proposition. To some extent I had anticipated their offer from my earlier correspondence with the King, and while still in Pondo Land had made a rough map of the route a road might follow from Port St. John's to Basutoland. I had discovered all the drifts in the rivers and all the traversable passes through the mountains. I had planned to transport the great stores of extra produce grown in Lerothodi's well-watered country over this route to Port St. John's. From there they could be taken to Cape Town on the Pedro Gorino. With a large concession in Basutoland and such a system for marketing my produce, I dreamed of gathering enough gold to help my race very materially. And there was always the possibility of a coalition of the Basutos and the Pondos, which would be one more step toward an Ethiopian Empire.

But it had been indiscreet to show them my entire hand, even to secure their promise of a loan. They had promised to back me to the extent of twenty thousand pounds if I secured such a concession and opened such a road as I had outlined, yet I felt strangely insecure and at their mercy.

During my stay in Cape Town I had arranged all my affairs, reconditioned my boat, and prepared for another absence. I had made Will Braithwaith Captain of the Pedro Gorino and had advanced the bos'n, an intelligent young West Indian, to the position of first mate. I had left much of my business in the hands of Price. And although even at the time, it had flashed across my mind that he had seemed a little too anxious to help, I had been reassured when I remembered his faithful work with Benjamin. I had stayed long enough to see the boat load, and make its departure for Delagoa Bay. Then satisfied that all was well, I had caught a train for Bloemfontein in the Orange River Colony, as near as I could come by rail to Lerothodi's kraal.

Now I was filled with apprehension. Little remarks that Price had made began to come back to me. They had meant nothing then, but they seemed significant now. I argued with myself that it was useless to worry. I thought of my many assets, my good-sized bank account, the Pedro Gorino piling up profit on every journey, my possibilities of a concession in Basutoland and the promise of backing to develop such a concession. Very soon now I would be in a position to do more for my race than any colored man before me. What could my enemies do except take my material wealth? They could not undermine the influence I was already gaining with the natives. They could not undo my work once I had instilled the desire for liberty in those fertile Ethiopian minds. I would attempt to lead my race toward a new goal. I might even hope to help counteract such disastrous influences on the natives as those Cecil Rhodes and his cohorts had brought to bear. By the time I reached my destination my mind was at rest.

I had informed Lerothodi and Queen Baring of my plan to visit their country, so when I disembarked at Bloemfontein a delegation of natives was awaiting my arrival. After I had had a good night's rest we all mounted our horses and proceeded towards Maseru, the King's kraal, some eighty miles distant.

In the region of the Caledon River we found the most picturesque country in South Africa. Everywhere there were mountains and cliffs and plume-like waterfalls on a hundred streams. I have seen Switzerland, but I prefer the country of the Basutos, for, while the views are scarcely as magnificent or vast, it offers a greater variety of scenery and is less spoiled and more wildly romantic. Single huts of stone and in places whole kraals cling miraculously to the cliffs. The veritable cliff-dwellers who inhabit these abodes are as agile and daring as klipspringers. Even the children we saw, ran and jumped along the narrow paths as if a misstep did not mean a fall of five hundred feet to certain death.

But the country is not all mountainous. Its great fields of mealies on the river bottoms and in the lower hills would almost entitle it to be called the granary of South Africa. Everywhere in the rougher country might be seen herds of cattle, sheep, goats and particularly horses, for the only horses the British will purchase are those bred in Basutoland.

I saw that this country was capable of a rich export in skins, hides, ostrich feathers, mohair, and grain. And when I realized that I had mapped a short cut to the sea, a road which with the expenditure of very little money would handle wagon-train-loads of produce, I knew that soon I would be independently wealthy.

When I arrived at Maseru I found it an almost impenetrable mountain stronghold built high on a cliff overlooking miles of rugged country. Here I was introduced to King Lerothodi and Queen Baring, a very handsome couple. The King was a stately looking, middle-aged man dressed in European fashion. The Queen was taller and more slender than the average native woman. She had a sensitive, intelligent face, and was an educated lady and a Christian. She wore Parisian dresses of pale yellow and green silks, and seemed a fitting mate for Lerothodi.

And then whom should I meet but Judge Con Rideout, an old friend of mine back in Mississippi. He wore a high silk hat and a Prince Albert coat even up there in the mountains. And he ran legal phraseology all through his conversations. In introducing me to his Basuto friends he would say, 'Inasmuch as you all have not heretofore met my esteemed friend and brother, Captain Harry Dean, nor the aforesaid Dean become acquainted with you all, I should like to make the presentments of each to the other and the other to each.' But we all have our idiosyncrasies, and Judge Con Rideout was an excellent man and a clever lawyer. He had helped King Lerothodi out of many difficulties with the English, had organized a parliamentary form of government in Basutoland, and occupied an important post in that government.

He accompanied me to the low, massive, stone house of the King whenever there was to be a conference over my plans in Basutoland. The King and Queen were always receptive, and before the first week had passed I had outlined my entire scheme. I offered to build the road to Port St. John's at my own expense and help to organize an adequate system of schools in return for any piece of land they wished to concede. I explained that I was not interested in personal gain and that everything I realized from a concession would be utilized in helping my race. The King was courteous but the Queen was actually enthusiastic. She and I had numerous talks upon these matters and I showed her how easily we might effect a coalition between the Pondos, the Pondo Mesis, and the Basutos. She was clever enough to see that her husband would be King over such a union.

With these and other things in mind she granted me

all her property on the Caledon River. The concession when developed would have been easily worth a million pounds sterling. While it gave me a fortune it also gave the Basutos several big advantages. Although they were the most powerful native nation in South Africa during the Boer War, they were no match for the Boers. To put the holdings of an American citizen between them and their old enemies more than counteracted their disadvantage. For as Lerothodi explained, although the Basutos could put many thousand men in the field their lack of guns handicapped them tremendously and their enemies' advantage was only to be neutralized by some such ruse as the one just employed.

There is no such thing as private property in Basutoland. I held my land, however, under the same right that the Queen had held it. By the native law it was mine. It was mine to cultivate and exploit, mine on which to pasture cattle or build cities. There was, of course, the enormous task of developing my holdings, but I felt certain that it was within my power.

My end of the bargain was not easy. I was to collect all the educators and builders I could persuade to come to Basutoland, and start them on the work of developing the country. We dreamed of a center from which culture could radiate to every corner of Africa. It was in the pursuance of this, the hunt for the right sort of men, that I started out over the trails of South Africa while the Boer War was still raging. Riding with one or two companions on horseback, daily I met with danger and adventure. And so it was I turned up in every village and kraal, karoo and veld, searching for men.

CHAPTER XXIII

A BATTLE WITH THE BOERS

From this point forward my adventures in Africa assumed a bright, illogical sequence with little rhyme or reason. I was traveling everywhere, combing the country for intelligent colonists to go to Basutoland. I received Segow Faku's permission to extend the road through his country. I wired Cape Town for materials to be shipped to Port St. John's via the Pedro Gorino. One by one the cogs in my great machine began to function.

The first man whom I was able to persuade to join my colony was a worthy young American from Georgia by the name of Douglas. The world in general is, perhaps, unaware of the manner in which the natives in South Africa are treated. At Bloemfontein and elsewhere they are segregated from the European element by confinement in compounds, where they are forced to wear collars and tags as if they were dogs in a kennel. Because he was a colored man Douglas had been forced to live in the compound at Bloemfontein and to submit to the humiliation of one of these dog-collars. Despite all his protests, and his frequent assertions that he was an American citizen, the authorities condemned him to live this prisoner-of-war type of life. I met him shortly after I had begun my travels in search of colonists, and I was so incensed at the story of tyranny which he related that I determined to secure his release. Although he had lost his papers I knew by the cut of his jib and the degree of his education that he was an American and that his story was true. I appealed to the American Consul and to five or six important officials at Bloemfontein and managed to secure his release. The matter was quickly hushed up, for the American government, while not thoroughly honorable in all respects, will seldom endure such insults to its citizens as those heaped upon Douglas. As this young man was an expert stone mason, I was anxious to get him for my project in Basutoland. He was very grateful for having been freed and readily accepted my proposition.

Incidentally I saw something of the Boer War in my travels. De Wet's raid on Cape Colony had been repulsed and the Boers had been driven back. They were now playing hide-and-seek with Ian Hamilton and General French.

These Boers were the toughest, most God-forsaken bunch of mortals the world has ever seen. They were for the most part low Dutch mixed with Hottentot with just enough American pirates, slavers, and highjackers added to imbue them with sin and love of the devil. The English robbed and mistreated the natives on every possible occasion, but the Boers, because they had no gentility and no antecedents whatsoever, outdid their neighbors in all forms of iniquity. There was, however, a certain romance about these men. These great coarse fellows with wide felt hats and bandannas about their necks were to be seen here and there in mounted detachments fighting valiantly enough, deluded though they were.

I was all through South Africa during the Boer War, but I did not see any real battles until I had left Bloemfontein and gone to Thabanchu, a town at the base of the impenetrable mountain, down which, in earlier years, the Basutos had rolled boulders upon their enemies, thus resisting attack after attack by English, Boers, and natives. Here at Thabanchu I had met again my old friend Lieutenant Garvin, an Australian-born Englishman, son of a big iron manufacturer. He was a graduate of Oxford and at this time an intelligence officer on the staff of Ian Hamilton. He was quite alone and scouting for news of the Boers. He asked me if I would like to accompany him, and since he would be able to get me through the lines to any point in South Africa not actually in the hands of the Boers, I accepted gladly. I was particularly anxious to go to Kimberley to see some men about my project, and since the army was moving in that general direction I saw that it would be to my advantage to accompany it.

We both had horses. When he had completed his work at Thabanchu, therefore, we put our belongings in our packs, mounted, and galloped away to join Ian Hamilton. After several hours of riding we came upon the English, who were encamped upon the veld fifty thousand strong.˙ They were out to capture De Wet, who was harassing them with his guerrilla warfare.

We spent the night among them and the next morning were up with the dawn. With admirable economy of effort and quiet orderliness this great army prepared to move forward. They formed eight columns at intervals of one half-mile each, so that the front ranks, which advanced simultaneously, stretched almost from horizon to horizon. Like an enormous comb it moved forward across the veld, and woe betide the unfortunate Boers caught in its teeth. Lieutenant Garvin and I were like two restless spirits. He was on special duty, accountable to no one but Hamilton himself and never obliged to stay with the columns. We traveled far out onto each flank and beyond into the open country and hills on either side, scouting for Boers.

On the third day out from Thabanchu, on the veld some distance northwest of Bloemfontein, while the columns moved forward in their typical formation, a shot was heard from a kopje directly before the right wing. I have never seen such perfect organization as that evinced by the British. The effect of the shot was immediate and certain. Within two minutes the eight columns were closing together as a fan closes and within an incredibly short time they were in solid formation half encircling the hill. The manner in which those men responded to the report of the Boer gun seemed to me to symbolize the whole internal organization of their country. No matter how much disharmony might occur among themselves, let a shot ring out or an enemy appear and they join forces and present a solid front just as they did on the plain that day. Sometimes it has been to such ignoble ends as reducing the natives and again it has been to do battle in a righteous cause.

The air was tense. No one knew whether there was one Boer or an army of many thousand men over the edge of that hill. Lieutenant Garvin and I rode our horses out to the right flank to get a better view of the country up ahead. Stationed upon a little rise we watched the maneuvers.

The whole army was in khaki even to the officers, for while red coats had been more romantic, the English had at last learned how impractical it was to make their men blazing targets for the enemies' guns. These khaki-clad figures almost blended into the veld, and I could imagine that at a distance they would be quite invisible to the naked eye.

The infantry was well ahead of the artillery, and before the guns could be rushed up the officers had ceased to ride back and forth giving orders to the Tommies and a great hush had fallen — a silence so intense as to be terribly depressing.

Then the three-inch guns, six to a battery, rolled up and took their positions. In another minute the bombardment had begun. The roaring of the guns and the bursting of shells was deafening. As we looked up toward the hills a mile away where the Boers were presumably hiding, we could see the crest nearest us literally blown to pieces. It seemed as if no living thing could exist in such a rain of steel. After fifteen minutes of this, Ian Hamilton gave a signal and the firing ceased and the infantry were ordered to attack. All along two miles they advanced, a solid line with fixed bayonets. The left and right wings, by encircling the hills, tried to outflank the enemy. With that purpose in mind our units advanced double-quick time.

Until this time there had been but the one shot from the Boers, and I thought it perfectly possible that the whole army was on a wild-goose chase. I was just contemplating how ridiculous they would feel on reaching the deserted hills, when Garvin, more experienced in this sort of warfare than I, explained the Boer technique. He thought it probable that the shot had been fired to bring the English into a solid formation, where more damage could be done with a few well-placed shots. The original report had come, he believed, from a point some distance from the actual position of the Boers. This would mislead a great deal of the English fire.

'But why are they silent now?' I asked.

'Their guns aren't particularly effective at this distance,' he said. 'You'll hear from them soon enough.'

The words were scarcely out of his mouth when the Boer artillery opened fire on the English lines which were now within a quarter-mile of the crest of the hills. In their two minutes of shelling nearly two hundred Tommies fell. The line never wavered, but plunged on up the steep incline. Then as miraculously as it had begun the firing ceased.

On our wing there was an English officer who was as immaculate as if he had been on parade at Aldershot. He wore a monocle and his uniform fairly shone. In one hand he carried a cane, for he limped slightly from some old wound or injury. His orders were given in a high feminine voice, 'Column right into line, march!' He had a perfect Oxford accent, but the pitch was an octave too high. We could scarcely conceal our amusement upon seeing this ladylike sample of London drawing-rooms fighting such a tough, hardy bunch as the Boers. He passed within twenty feet of us and just as he came abreast one of the last shells the Boers fired fell half-way between his column and the little knoll where we were sitting upon our horses. It threw up a great cloud of dust, but bounded another seventy-five feet before exploding. No one was hurt, but the officer's uniform was dirtied. He pulled a white handkerchief from his pocket, flicked away the dust, and said so audibly that we could hear him, 'Fawncy that, this beastly dust.'

We could not refrain from laughing outright, but we did not miss the fact that he was a brave man and had not shown the least concern at his narrow escape.

A few moments later we galloped off, and circling the right wing reached the top of the kopje only a few moments after the first of the infantry. As Lieutenant Garvin had predicted, most of the English fire had been misdirected by the simple ruse of the Boers. Some two hundred dead, in all their rough romantic garb, were lying on the ground, and a dead Boer because of his size and dress looks like three dead Tommies, but not a live enemy was in sight. In a protected spot a short distance away we found the hoofprints of some thousand horses that had been tethered there. Six or seven old-fashioned field-guns had been abandoned. But with the exception of these signs of recent activity, there was no way of telling that hundreds of Boers had been there ten minutes before. They had slipped away on their fast horses down a dry ravine to the northeast, and although a detachment of cavalry was sent to overtake them, the Boers soon lost themselves in the wild country with which they were so familiar, and left the English far behind.

The next morning when the army was again prepared to move forward, Garvin was given the order to precede the columns by several miles, watching the hills for any sign of the enemy. He and I set forth at daybreak and traveled along a road which wound down a fertile little valley with hills on either side. A clear stream bubbled along beside us and on either hand might be seen the orchards of the Boer farmers. The weather was clear and exhilarating, yet warm enough for comfort. It was almost impossible to believe that a war was in progress, for nothing could have been more peaceful than this pastoral scene.

Several times during the morning we dismounted and examined the ground closely, but there was nothing to indicate that a large body of men had recently passed this way. Occasionally we left the road and went to the crest of near-by hills to view the surrounding country. It was always with the same result, nothing of interest within the range of our binoculars. At one point we came upon a little Boer of seven or eight fishing in the stream. We asked him if men had recently passed this way, but he was so frightened that he never uttered a word, but dove headlong into a patch of willow growth and hid there like a terrified little animal.

By middle afternoon we had grown a bit careless and were riding down the road laughing and talking. But as our conversation came around to the war again, Garvin suddenly became more serious. 'You know,' he said, 'it would be strange if right now within a few months of the end some Boer took a pot shot at me. I've taken as many chances as a man can and I've come out without a scratch. But somehow this afternoon I have a premonition of trouble.' I tried to cheer him up in every way I knew, but for almost an hour he was very quiet and seemed to be deep in thought. It troubled me, for Garvin was usually the most light-hearted of men.

It was within an hour of sunset when we reached a bend of the highway hidden by mimosa and willow growth. Beyond this bend the road wound up a low range of kopjes. These hills, together with the over-hanging trees, made a perfect setting for an ambuscade. Suddenly from the hills and trees which were on our right a volley of fifty shots rang out. The bullets poured into us like rain. Once again Garvin had been right in his prediction, and that brave fellow fell to the ground with a bullet through his heart. His horse, which had been mortally wounded, plunged and fell to the ground tearing up the gravel of the highway in his agony. I was untouched, but my horse had been badly wounded in the flank. This and the sound of the shots, and the other animal pawing the gravel so terrified him that he swerved and raced back down the road almost throwing me from the saddle. There was no way of controlling my wounded mount, so I merely let him have a free rein and hung on. I thought mournfully of the once light-hearted Garvin lying dead in the road and I hoped against hope that the English could capture or kill every one of those Boers. A few minutes later I reached the column and was able to get my beast under control. I informed the first officer at hand of the Boer ambush up ahead. A unit of cavalry was immediately dispatched. But although these men rode like the wind toward the scene of the disaster they found no trace of the Boers. They recovered the body of Garvin, however, which was given every honor and subsequently shipped to his grief-stricken father in Australia.

CHAPTER XXIV

DIAMOND KINGS AND DIAMOND SMUGGLERS

A FEW days later I reached Kimberley. Almost the first man I met upon my arrival was Kid Gardener, and he seemed as debonair as ever. He had finally been released from prison and some weeks before had come to the diamond country to join Haji Hassan. He appeared to be more prosperous than an English Lord, and I determined once and for all to uncover his mysterious source of income.

I asked him point blank, 'Kid, what's your game?'

He pulled out a big uncut diamond, flipped it into the air with his thumb, and returned it to his vest pocket. 'That's my game,' he said.

So that was it. He was diamond smuggling, was he? I was keenly interested and quite unable to conceal my curiosity. At first he was wary, but as the days passed he disclosed to me the greatest diamond smuggling outfit in South Africa. He offered me a chance to make a tremendous fortune if I could overcome my scruples. He and Haji Hassan had the smoothest little system I have ever seen. Haji was the master mind of the organization and controlled all the business from Mafeking, where in daily life he played the rôle of an illiterate Malay. To allay suspicion he ran a small grocery store where his trade amounted to some thirty shillings a day. The Kid was Haji's Kimberley agent and therefore his right-hand man. But Haji had five hundred others in his employ, scattered through all the diamond diggings in South Africa, and a system of runners who traveled at night over the unfrequented paths of veld, karoo, and jungle — natives who knew every inch of the country and could be trusted with a pouch of stones worth fifty thousand pounds.

And Haji Hassan sat on the porch of his grocery store in Mafeking, dozing through the warm afternoons, talking to his occasional customers, or spelling out the words of the evening paper (and he the greatest Arabian scholar in Africa). Little did the English dream that here was the man for whose capture they were spending thousands of pounds a year. Nor did it avail the officials to take his agents and his runners; they were in honor bound never to betray Haji, and if the Kid knew the real facts in the case Haji was never in danger of capture but once.

That had been much earlier in his career when he had been controlling his organization from Port Elizabeth. In those days he had taken more chances. His wife, a beautiful Malay girl, used to slip aboard the boats that came to the harbor and offer the European passengers stones at a price far below that which they would have to pay elsewhere. For almost two years she was successful in escaping detection. But a jealous woman betrayed her and one day Haji's wife was arrested and thrown into prison. Her bail was set at one hundred thousand pounds, which Haji was able to furnish only by sacrificing most of his fortune. Once he had her safe outside the prison walls he lost no time in putting her aboard a ship bound for Arabia. The bail was, of course, forfeited and Haji spent the rest of his days separated from his wife; but he at least knew that he had done the only honorable thing.

As the Kid told me of Haji and of the fortunes awaiting successful smugglers I was tempted to join forces with these men. Why not? What right had the English to exploit a country that by every natural law belonged to the Ethiopian race? Why should we not try to regain our own? They all were smugglers and thieves when you came right down to it. Even Gardener Williams, superintendent of the De Beers mines, indulged in piracy now and then. He played his own particular rôle in the raid on the Transvaal, and if that attack by John Hays Hammond, Dr. Jameson and their army of mercenaries was not as thorough a case of brigandage as the pampered sons of imperialism ever attempted, I do not know villainy when I see it. But the Boers beat them at their own game and made the hirelings scatter like leaves before the four winds. And because his brother was among them, Cecil Rhodes had to pay Paul Krüger a million pounds if he paid him a shilling to keep that wily Boer from executing half a dozen of the most picturesque and bloodthirsty freebooters Africa has ever seen. No, one gets but few of the actual facts on such matters. They had to save Jameson's reputation, and Gardener Williams's reputation, and Cecil Rhodes's reputation, and the reputation of the British Government, and after that there was little of the truth they dared let slip. There is no use of my risking my life by telling what I know.

When I also remembered how the English had robbed the natives of Griqualand West of their diamond mines, and passed laws which made it legal for their powerful courts to condemn these same natives to life imprisonment if an uncut diamond was ever found in their possession, even my affiliations with the African Methodist Episcopal Church scarcely served to keep me from joining Haji Hassan and Kid Gardener. My sentiments were those of the Africando sentenced to seventeen years on the Breakwater for finding a diamond beside his own doorstep when he said, 'Dis a fruit dat grow in my country. Why you say, "no pick"?'

The Kid could see that I was interested, and since I had befriended him in the past he let me in on many of the secrets. There were several ways of smuggling diamonds out of the mines of South Africa. Each race had its own method, but Haji Hassan had the safest and surest system. The mines were worked by natives under contract to serve for a stipulated period of time. Every few months it was necessary to recruit new labor from the kraals. Shortly before the recruitment in any particular kraal Haji would plant several of his confidential men, strip them of all outward signs of civilization, array them as the natives themselves and leave the rest of the deception to their own intelligence. These men could appear every bit as unsophisticated as the natives, and although the De Beers agents were continually on the watch they were deceived over and over again. After they had been employed and taken to the mines, they awaited their chance. The mines are heavily guarded and surrounded by high fences of barbed wire. It is absolutely impossible for an outsider to get in and out of the properties. To further complicate matters the employees are made to live within the guarded fences.

None of these difficulties worried Haji. Once his men were inside he secured just such daring, brilliant fellows as the Kid to complete his system. The Texan was absolutely trusted by Gardener Williams, who thought him a fine type of American 'negro' and allowed him to accompany sight-seers and now and then guide parties through the mines. The rest was comparatively simple. By legerdemain the men inside slipped the Kid the diamonds they had secreted about their persons. He would sometimes leave the mines with half a dozen big stones. One afternoon he showed me a pouch containing fifty.

Because of the danger of holding the uncut stones, runners were dispatched every few days to Haji Hassan at Mafeking. When his hidden treasure-boxes held the accumulation of several weeks of plunder from among the various mines of South Africa, he would prepare a shipment for transportation to a firm in Amsterdam, Holland, with which he did all his business. He had a particularly faithful runner with whom he entrusted this packet, who covered the distance between Mafeking and Delagoa Bay in remarkably short time considering the rough, unfrequented paths over which he ran.

One trick which saved Haji's men more than once was an old ruse indeed, but a successful one. Every runner and agent in his employ was given orders to swallow his stones if close pressed. Even Kid Gardener was forced to resort to this on a number of occasions. . . .

My acquaintanceship in Kimberley was not limited to diamond smugglers, however. I had heard that Gardener Williams was a Californian, and so one day I decided to approach him. He was a very gentlemanly fellow and had I not known his past I might have been inclined to disbelieve the stories concerning his hard, crafty nature. He had known my uncle Solomon in California and he treated me very civilly indeed. I became well acquainted with him during my stay in Kimberley, and one afternoon he invited me to come to his office to see a collection of stones he had gathered.

We entered the unpretentious brick buildings that housed the offices of the De Beers diamond mines. He went to the enormous safe which filled one wall of the room, gave the dial a whirl, threw back the forty-ton doors, and removed from its shelf a collection of diamonds which for some years was considered the finest in the world. The tray was five feet square lined with green velvet and on its surface as thickly scattered as dewdrops on a field of clover were fifteen or sixteen hundred, purest water diamonds. The afternoon sun which fell through the window shone and glittered on the great tray of treasure.

And there within my reach was wealth enough to found the Ethiopian Empire of which I had dreamed so long. Three feet away was a hoard which would have civilized and educated half the natives of Africa, all gathered into one heap for a single man's pleasure. There were diamonds on that tray of every shape and size but all of the same purity. There were pear-shaped diamonds and diamonds cut in diverse ways.

Some were only two or three carats and some must have been fifty. I wanted to plunge my hands into the treasure and go forth and free Africa. I wanted to alter the course of destiny and administer justice in my own way. It would have been useless. I would have been shot down before I could have gone a hundred yards.

Then the fever for diamonds filled me and I was as mad for treasure as the thousands who had gone before me. The wild excitement that has lured men across seas and continents, into freezing wildernesses, and through steaming jungles engulfed me. I had money, so I bought a diamond machine, an invention which washes the diamonds from the dirt in the alluvial deposits. I hired natives. I went before the officials and was allotted a claim near the Vaal River. I arranged for the purchase of water and early one morning transported all of my equipment to the desolate, boulder-strewn country where men labor year after year in search of little stones and cry for joy when one is found.

Soon we were washing tons of conglomerate filled with bantams, a small round stone which invariably appears in the region of diamonds. The dirt was full of garnets and semi-precious stones. Every few minutes one of the men would find one. We must have picked up a pint of these in the first week, but not one diamond rewarded our search. I was not to be discouraged, however. I urged the natives to even greater efforts by promising them more pay with an extra reward to the man who could find a stone. On the tenth day we found our first diamond, a fine sixteen-carat stone which cut would have brought many hundred dollars in the right market. But the licensed buyers, locally known as 'kopje-wallopers,' to whom we were forced to sell, gave us but sixteen pounds. The find cheered us greatly, however, and seemed to have changed our luck for from that day forth we took diamonds from the dirt with satisfying regularity.

I had been in this country several weeks and had made a considerable amount of money when fortune began to turn against me. Kid Gardener came to me one day entirely out of funds. For a long time his smuggling had been completely successful, but recently he was being watched. One sentence on the Breakwater had made him wary, and on this occasion he knew enough to stop before it was too late. A week before when he had delivered his last pouch of diamonds he had had a small fortune. Since that time he had gambled heavily and lost every shilling of it. I gave him money and he was often to be seen about my diggings.

Whether the English grew to hate me because the Kid was in my company, or whether it was their usual grievance against my presence in South Africa, the fact that they felt I was a dangerous character and an organizer of the Ethiopian Movement, I do not know. But certainly they began to harass me in every possible way. One of the devices often used to trap the unsuspecting small operator is to send a native to him with an unregistered rough diamond, with the hope that he will purchase the stone and thus throw himself open to immediate arrest. I was told a day in advance that the English intended to play this trick on me.

When I told the Kid what I had learned he explained how I might out-trick them. 'Listen, Captain, when de boy comes wid dat stone, grab it and pretend as how you've t'rown it clear 'cross de river, den snap it up yo' sleeve and cuss him out of yo' diggin's fast as he can travel. Den as far as de bulls know yo' ain't got no stone and when night comes yo' put it wid de rest and get 'em all registered.'

The next morning several Englishmen came to my diggings and wandered about asking questions and examining the soil. I knew well enough what they were up to, but I pretended not to notice them. About ten o'clock a native with a suspiciously good command of English came and offered to sell me a beautiful big uncut diamond. The Englishmen gathered around as though mildly interested. I snatched the stone from his fingers and pretended to throw it far out among the boulders; in reality I snapped it up my sleeve, where it remained until I had an opportunity to remove it.

At first the Englishmen were amazed, then they were furious. They had lost a big diamond and had been cheated out of the pleasure of arresting me. They were unable to conceal their displeasure and I knew that my trouble had only started. I was right in this surmise, for two days later I found a diamond 'planted' in my cot. I removed it hurriedly, fully realizing what to expect. Less than a half hour later our camp was literally torn to pieces by officers searching for unregistered stones. My cot was kicked over and the bedding ripped to shreds. One of the Englishmen who had been at my diggings on the day the first trick had been attempted, was so angry that his face was contorted with rage. 'I'll get you if it takes me the rest of my life,' he said.

I knew that the time had come for my departure. The imperialists, not satisfied with unlawfully seizing a country, exterminating great numbers of the male population, virtually enslaving those who remained, and reducing the whole race to abject poverty, had become so jealous of their stolen wealth that they were unwilling to let an Ethiopian acquire even that part of the treasure which their own unjust laws allowed.

I sold my outfit at a loss, paid off my help, and prepared to leave the country as quickly as possible, taking with me sixteen unregistered stones, of which the two best were the ones the English had so grudgingly given me. The Kid made a run for Johannesburg where he was later murdered. So he is where this evidence will never be held against him, gone back to the dust of his motherland, where I hope some day to lie.

CHAPTER XXV

THE SWAZIS AND THE ZULUS GO TO WAR

MY search for men continued. I went to far cities and strange regions. And so it was that one day I came to the Boer village of Piet Retief and because I had been journeying many days decided to rest over Sunday. This village was little more than a cluster of Boer farms, but I was able to hire accommodations for myself and beast and to pass a day and night most pleasantly. I had been prepared to leave upon the following morning when by singular coincidence I met my old friend Donald Hawkins, foreign correspondent for a London newspaper. He had taken a room in the farmhouse at which I was staying, and when I had come down to the evening meal I had found him sitting beside me. We greeted each other in happy surprise, but our words were cut short by the three-hundred-pound Boer at the head of the table, who held up his hand for silence and informed us that he was about to thank God for the food before us and he did not want to wait all evening as he was hungry.

These Boers are the laziest and most hypocritical people I have ever seen. All that this old fellow ever did was to sit upon his front porch reading the Bible and drinking quarts of coffee, but for all his religion he abused the natives in his employ most unmercifully. A Kaffir boy was fanning this enormous man while he dragged on and on through a grace which lasted fully ten minutes. The droning words almost put the lad to sleep and for a moment the fanning ceased. The Boer stopped in the middle of his blessing, turned upon the boy and cursed him roundly, then returned to the labor of thanking God for the food before us. Hawkins and I could scarcely suppress our laughter; in fact the eyes of the newspaper man fairly streamed tears in his effort to remain composed.

When the meal was over and we were by ourselves I had an opportunity to ask him what he was doing in this country. He had arrived in South Africa over a year before to 'cover' the Boer War, but at this moment he was after other material. 'Surely you know that the Swazis and the Zulus have gone to war,' he said.

I had to admit that I had heard only faint rumor of trouble. I had had no idea that it had come to actual war. Hawkins invited me to accompany him on the following day when he was planning to ride to a point some thirty miles distant, where it was reputed that two enormous native armies were gathering to do battle. I accepted gladly and the next morning we saddled our horses and set out for the battlefield.

As we rode along, we talked of native warfare and of the reasons for friction among the natives. Pro-British though he was, he agreed with me when I said, 'I am fully convinced that the Boers and the English have the same attitude toward the natives. I believe that when they see it would be to their own advantage to weaken two tribes by putting them at war with one another, neither these bastard Dutchmen nor your own blue-blooded friends in His Majesty's service hesitate one moment.' We both understood, however, that there was a second reason for this trouble, which sprang indirectly out of the Boer War. Many of the Zulu boys were hired as drivers by the Boers and the English. Neither side would let them carry guns, for teaching them the use of firearms was the last thing in the world they wished to do. But since for driving horses, mules, or oxen these boys were unsurpassed, many were employed in this capacity. The result, however, was very detrimental to the young natives, weakening their tribal customs and morals without giving them a new set to take the place of those they were losing. This and the proximity of Swaziland led to promiscuity with Swazi girls. The two tribes were ready to cut each other to pieces at a moment's notice, and we realized that we were about to witness an important battle.

We had proceeded some fifteen miles out of Piet Retief when a most extraordinary occurrence quite detracted our attention from the Swazi-Zulu trouble. We had been thirsty, and seeing a spring bubbling from the rocks had tied our horses to a convenient tree and descended some distance down a gradual incline into a ravine at the bottom of which the spring was located.

After we had quenched our thirst we stood looking at the pleasantly uneven country on either hand and talking of the great inroads made on the big game of South Africa. 'For instance,' I said, 'while there were rhinoceroses all through this country some years ago there isn't one within a hundred miles of us now. I've seen plenty of them north of the Limpopo but they are all cleaned out down here.'

Suddenly Hawkins silenced me and pointed to a

small clump of bushes a hundred yards down the ravine. 'Isn't that a rhino lying there?' he asked.

'Quite impossible,' I said. 'You would be as likely to see one on the streets of Cape Town.'

Hawkins was not to be satisfied, however, so I laughingly consented to go with him and investigate. I had had a good deal of experience with these big, ill-tempered animals and I knew that despite their poor eyesight they are dangerous beasts and best left alone. Their senses of smell and of hearing are so acute that their charges are often fatal.

I felt that we would find nothing but a big gray boulder when we reached the brush, yet instinctively I noticed that we were down wind from the quarry. At seventy-five yards I saw that I had been mistaken. We were able to get a much better view, and Hawkins had been right. There lay a rhino, and a big one, of the variety known as 'black.' I had just whispered that we had better not disturb him, when some little noise we had made reached him. His ears stiffened, he rose to his feet, sniffed the air and charged.

A man who has never had one of these beasts charge down upon him has no conception of the way we felt. This animal had all the appearances of an infuriated locomotive, and his two wicked horns seemed as dangerous as a dozen bayonets. The speed at which he moved was amazing. Our horses were three hundred feet away. To reach them or to outrun the beast was unthinkable. There was no tree into which we might swing ourselves. We could do nothing but meet the charge. Each of us had a revolver and I had a rifle slung across my back. But at this moment when a wasted second meant disaster I seemed quite unable to unloose the rifle. For a few moments I continued to struggle, then seeing that it was useless I drew my revolver. Each armed with his puny weapon we awaited the chance to place close enough shots to be even slightly effective. I had seen rhinos turned with a heavy charge of buckshot and I had seen them come right on after being hit with the ball from a six hundred. There was no way of knowing what this one might do. But I felt certain we could not turn him. There is no accounting for the idiosyncrasies of individual animals, however. We opened fire on this rhinoceros at fifteen yards. He hesitated, amazed; then galloped up out of the ravine and away.

The rest of the day I took great care not to be dogmatic, for fear Hawkins might remind me of the rhinoceros we had found in a country where there were no rhinoceroses.

When we reached the point where the two armies were reputed to be facing each other ready for battle, we found three or four thousand Swazis drawn into line at the top of a low range of kopjes, awaiting attack. In the valley below them, some two miles away, were the Zulus, ten thousand strong.

The Zulu army was drawn into the typical bull-horn formation which I had noticed in Pondo Land. Occasionally during the afternoon one of these horns would advance toward the enemy a half-mile or so, but invariably it would retreat again. Sometimes the two horns alternated in this advance and retreat until I could imagine a great bull fencing, this way and that, with vicious thrusts.

The natives were armed with knobkerries and assegais. They had shields of various shapes and colors to protect them from the onslaught of the enemy. Each army had eight or ten rifles, smuggled at the risk of life and limb from the English and the Boers. The men were dressed in paint and feathers with red, blue, and white clay upon their faces. They were so hideous and phantastic in this array that they seemed scarcely human; rather they were the symbol of hate. Yet these same men were kindly and generous in days of peace.

We joined a small trek train of farmers and freighters who were drawn together in an encampment for the night. From this vantage point we watched the armies through our glasses, knowing that at any time the battle might begin. As evening approached great fires were built by both armies. Dancing and howling, beating of drums and wild singing disturbed the usually quiet air. Messages, no doubt of a very insulting nature, were carried back and forth all night long, until by morning the excitement and anger of these men were at a white heat.

At this point, however, a new element entered the struggle. Before the sun had fully risen a Boer officer and his commando arrived upon the field. They took an advantageous position to the north of us, a little less than two miles from either army. The native armies, each of which was worked to battle pitch, did not attack each other. They realized the sinister meaning of that Boer commando. Likewise Hawkins and I understood. These Boers had come to fight the winning army. Not satisfied with setting tribes upon each other to weaken the natives wherever possible, they often brought their own armies to the battlefields to whip the tired victors.

For hours the three armies held their positions without moving an inch. No messages were sent; nothing happened; but we could feel the air fairly alive with hatred, fear, and desire for blood.

Sometimes it seems to me that in emotional matters natives are blind to reason. The Zulus were well aware of the intention of the Boers, yet before the sun was half way up the heavens the Zulu chiefs were again working their men to a high pitch of excitement. This time they had to overcome not only the fear of the enemy but the fear of the Boers as well. It was necessary to play upon the emotions of these men until they were blind to everything but their own anger. As we watched them through our glasses we saw the Zulu chiefs speaking to their men quietly at first, then more loudly and more loudly until they were wildly shouting, and we could hear the noise even from where we watched. Then the singing, howling, horn-blowing and drum-beating began. By noon both native armies were lashed into such a passion that the excitement heretofore was mild by comparison.

Suddenly the wing of the Zulus which was nearest us advanced. Led by the King it rushed up the hill toward the staunch Swazis. The King waited until he was within fifty yards of the enemy, and then with a tremendous swing hurled his assegai. This was the formal declaration of war, and the battle was on. There was an advance all along the Zulu line and ten thousand black warriors shining in the sun surged up the hill to the attack. Each held his shield before him and howled in defiance as he fought.

For an hour the battle continued. The Swazi position was rushed again and again, but always the Zulus were repulsed by the foe who were less than half their number. Many were killed and many more wounded. Some of those hit by knobkerries in the first rush were on their feet and fighting again before the battle was over. From the moment of attack, however, the battle went to the Swazis, and at last these intrepid fighters poured down from the hill they had so successfully defended and cut the Zulu army squarely in two. The Zulus wavered, then broke and ran. Some of them came to our little encampment for shelter.

At this moment the Boer commando rode into battle, for just as we had surmised, it was their captain's purpose to whip the victor. These well-armed and mounted men swept down upon the defenseless Swazis, never coming within the range of the poor weapons the natives used. And without suffering a casualty themselves, the Boers fired volley after volley into the naked black ranks, killing scores and never giving quarter even to the wounded. They killed the natives as if they had been so many antelope and those brave warriors continued to fight their hopeless fight until half their number lay dead upon the plain. Then with a last volley of assegais they retreated into the hills, pursued by the Boers, who came thundering after them on their horses, pouring a stream of lead into their backs.

Half an hour later when we were preparing to leave,

the Boers were just returning. Incredible as it may seem they actually bragged about the afternoon's work. They called the wholesale murder they had committed a victory, and told of the fierceness of the natives and what luck it was that they had suffered no losses at the hands of these wild, black fellows. As a matter of fact, these Boers had been in no more danger than the middle-aged sportsmen who hunt ducks on their private marshes back in England and America.

Donald Hawkins was anxious to get his story in shape and on its way. Therefore, although it was night and the country rough, we rode the entire thirty miles back to Piet Retief, where we were able to get several hours of much-needed sleep.

CHAPTER XXVI

BLACK MAGIC IN THE BASUTO MOUNTAINS

I HAD sent a number of men up to my Caledon River concession, so after the battle between the Swazis and the Zulus I went to Basutoland to see how matters were shaping themselves and to confer with Queen Baring and King Lerothodi in regard to my work. I rode somewhat leisurely through that well-watered, mountainous country, for the past weeks had been exciting and strenuous. The streams were running so high that I had difficulty in crossing them at the drifts. In every valley horses and cattle grazed. Because I held land in this region, the abounding fertility filled me with a deep satisfaction.

The land reminded me of Scotland with its hills and herds, its meadows and streams. I was thinking of this as I approached Maseru, the King's kraal, built of stone and mortar high on a cliff. I was thinking that it was not so long ago that the proud Scots were building strongholds no less crude in a country similar to this, and that there was no reason why development should be slower among these people than it had been elsewhere in the world.

The King and Queen received me very graciously, as they expected great results from my project in Basutoland. Douglas, the American whom I had found at Bloemfontein, had started building three stone houses on my concession. As they were not yet completed, the Queen offered me one of her houses in which to live until I could move into a house of my own. I hired a boy named Nizie to do my work, and having accepted the Queen's hospitality prepared to spend a season at Maseru.

Nizie was a short, heavy-set, dark brown fellow with fine big eyes and white teeth that showed when he smiled, which was a great deal of the time. He was a very quiet and efficient servant, with a devotion for me which was quite touching. Although he was uneducated and slow-witted he was thoroughly dependable. I had no idea that he would be the innocent agent of another's black magic, or that within these peaceful walls disaster hung over me like a sword.

Some of my men were already at Maseru and others arrived every few days. The first of my materials and supplies had come via the Pedro Gorino to Port St. John's, and from that point over the mountains via trek train. Work began in earnest. I rode all over my great concession, planned a town with many buildings, examined the soil, the forests of South African hardwood, and the river itself and where it might be forded. I drew a rough map of my land to scale, showing the points at which the best timber and the best stone could be secured for building.

Some of the land was clear, and fell in gently rolling hills and meadows toward the river. This country was perfect for grazing, and I planned to put herds of horses and cattle upon it in the near future. Other parts of the concession were steep and rocky, covered with a thick growth of timber. One hill rose abruptly from the valley floor to a height of nine hundred feet. Several streams wound across my land to feed the rapid river, and springs of pure water insured a supply the year round for drinking. I planned for orchards and vineyards and superintended the work on the buildings, which went forward rapidly.

Any morning when the dew was on the grass I could go out with my shotgun and almost without taking aim shoot enough doves for dinner. The river was filled with fish, and buck were plentiful.

One day as I was riding along the river bank I sighted a herd of seventy or eighty wild ostriches. I could have ordered my men to capture them and pluck them since they were on my land, but I decided first to ask Queen Baring's permission. She gave it readily and ordered a hundred of her boys to help me in the work.

We herded every ostrich on my concession into one great kraal and began our work. Wild ostriches, strange to say, are often better tempered than tame ones, and we had very little difficulty. An ostrich can administer a kick fatal to man, but when a small kaross of skins is thrown over his head he will stand perfectly still and allow his captors to pluck his feathers. We secured two large wooden cases and in these we packed our treasure. We took only the black and the white wing-feathers of the cock birds, and by careful selection throughout the great herd we were able to obtain the finest shipment of feathers I have ever seen. Some of the primes at a conservative estimate were worth a sovereign apiece. I wanted to share my plunder with the Queen, but she insisted that I keep it all myself. I had had some experience with ostrich feathers and I knew that this lot which I shipped to Cape Town to await my return was worth approximately five thousand pounds sterling.

Despite these strokes of good fortune my visit was destined to be an unhappy one, for it was in this remote and secluded part of South Africa that the British made one of their most dastardly attempts at my life. Perhaps once again it was diamonds that aroused their jealousy. I had found every indication of both gold and diamonds on my concession and I confided my discoveries to King Lerothodi. In return for this confidence he took me to another part of Basutoland and showed me three of the richest diamond prospects in South Africa. We both knew that to mention a word concerning the wealth hidden in these mountains would be the first step toward losing our land and we agreed to keep our knowledge a secret. But as everywhere else in South Africa, here in Basutoland there were ears trained for every whisper, eyes watching every movement.

Thus it was that the agent of the high imperialists, Old S——, received knowledge of my hidden wealth. Afraid that I might acquire a shilling that he and his cohorts desired, he went into conference with the devil, and those two wicked old rascals conceived a most hellish plan.

Here are the facts as I learned them some months later. Old S—— had called to his aid a crafty native, whom he controlled body and soul, and having handed him a sealed vial together with complete instructions, had sent him into the interior of Basutoland. This native mounted his horse and two days later arrived at Maseru. I noticed the appearance of a strange face about the kraal, but thought nothing of it. When this fellow started to become friendly with Nizie, however, I grew interested. There was something about the man that made me shiver. He had a long bullet scar on one cheek, bloodshot eyes, and thin lips. It was a face I had seen before, but I could not remember where. His presence about the kraal gave me a feeling of apprehension. I determined to ask Nizie about the fellow that very evening. The matter slipped my attention, however, and because I did not see the native again I forgot him entirely.

Some days later word came from Cape Town that the Prince of Wales, now King of England, was coming to South Africa. The Kings of all the tribes were invited to meet him at one huge reception. Almost simultaneously I received word from Segow Faku, King of the Pondos, saying that he alone of all South African potentates was to be barred from seeing the prince. I felt as he did that there was only one explanation. The colonial officials were afraid that some information regarding their cold-blooded conduct in Pondo Land might come to the notice of the Prince of Wales, and they were taking no chances. I was incensed at their high-handed attitude, and determined that after I had eaten my dinner I would dispatch letters to Segow Faku and Cape Town, seeing what might be done about the situation.

I sat down to the meal and as usual was served by Nizie. It seemed that he lingered over his serving, but the fact held no particular significance. I ate heartily as was my custom. On arising, however, I was taken with a giddy, faint feeling unlike anything I had ever experienced. I told myself that it would last only a moment, but the dizziness increased until the whole room was a blur before my eyes. Then my head began to ache frightfully, there was a roaring in my ears and a throbbing at my temples. I called in a native doctor who lived in the kraal. He was unable to tell the nature of my sickness, but honest enough to admit it. He gave me some medicine to soothe my headache and promised to stay within the kraal so that I could find him at any time.

I took the concoction, but continued to feel worse and worse. I spent a terrible night groaning and tossing and sinking away into delirium. Nizie watched beside my bed with great sad eyes and waited upon me all night long. The next morning I began to grow numb. The numbness crept up my arms and legs until I knew I was going to die. A yellow glaze came over my eyes and the whole world seemed strangely discolored. I called in the doctor again and he listened to my symptoms. He still was unable to diagnose my case, but he was sure that the only way to save my life was to rush me to Bloemfontein, where I could secure better medical aid. Suddenly the truth came to me. I knew that I had been poisoned. I called to my boy and said to him, 'Don't be afraid, Nizie, but tell me the truth. What did the man with the bad face give you to put in my food?'

Poor Nizie trembled like a leaf and rolled his big eyes. All that he could say was, 'Fella do it, fella do it.'

English was still very foreign to him and in his fright and grief he forgot the few words he knew. Luckily the doctor knew both Basuto and English and was able to translate for me. Nizie told the story brokenly in his own tongue, his voice betraying the sorrow that he felt.

It seems that the stranger had asked Nizie if he loved his master and if his master was a good man. Nizie who was very devoted to me had, of course, proclaimed his affection. The schemer had then instilled within this boy's brain the idea that he was in danger of being discharged. Nizie had asked if there was not some way the catastrophe could be diverted. This was the opening the scar-faced native wanted. He had given Nizie the 'love powder' in the vial to be administered secretly. And Nizie, thinking to keep my love, had poisoned me.

I forgave the boy and told him that if he would run and fetch a cart from the Boers on the far side of the Caledon River all would be well again. He went, and in an impossibly short period of time returned with the cart and a team of mules. He must have ridden his horse across country and have swum the river, for he could not have taken the longer route by road nor waited to reach a drift where he could have forded in safety. I took no notice of it then. Time meant life and death, yet to my clouded brain it meant nothing at all. I do remember some things clearly, however. I can still see Nizie as he stood watching my departure after Douglas and a Basuto boy had come to drive me to Bloemfontein. He was a perfect picture of dejection, his head hung and his shoulders drooping.

For a while I was painfully aware of the rough road over which we were traveling and the terrible pace.

Then somewhere along the way I lost consciousness. Perhaps it was hours or perhaps days before I awoke again. My dreams were filled with rivers and jungles. I lived over again the night in the bay at Knysna and again I was swimming for ever and ever without approaching a shore. I was being devoured slowly by a lion who shoved his hideous face into my own. But above all, my dreams were filled with a native whose cheek was scarred and whose eyes were small and bloodshot. . . .

At last I awoke. I was between white sheets in a comfortable bed. Some one was putting liquid into my mouth with a spoon and soothing my forehead. When I had recovered sufficiently to understand the words of the woman nursing me, I found that I was in the home of a colored doctor who had saved my life by his quick thinking. He was a West Indian with a Scottish medical education and probably the only man in Bloemfontein sufficiently skilled to have pulled me through. The woman who was caring for me was his wife. Douglas returned to Maseru as soon as he saw that I would recover, but I remained with the doctor and his wife for many days while I was convalescing. I was very grateful to these people and became attached to them because of their kindness. At last I was able to leave and proceed wearily for Cape Town. But I was not fully cured, for the effects of that poison are with me to-day.

CHAPTER XXVII
THE MEETING OF THE KINGS

CAPE TOWN was wild with excitement. I had arrived at noon two days before the Prince of Wales and I had found the city decorated with flowers and flags. A bright canopy had been spread over the section of the dock on which the Prince would land. Soon rugs of velvet were being laid on every inch of ground the royal feet might touch. The celebrating began a whole day before his arrival.

On the eventful morning I went to the dock to see the Prince come ashore. With the whole British Oriental fleet from its headquarters at Simon's Town for an escort, his ship steamed into Table Bay. A thousand flags and pennants fluttered in the sunshine. Guns on the ships and guns on shore fired salute after salute. All the high officials in South Africa from Sir Alfred Milner down were on the dock to greet him when he landed. But when the Prince came ashore, for all his braids and fine demeanor, I thought him no more royal or aristocratic than Segow Faku, his shining black body adorned with nothing but a breech-clout, an ostrich feather, and a necklace of ivory.

After the reception on the dock, the Prince was driven up Adderley Street with plumed horses, outriders, and a huge military guard. The carriage took him through the Gardens to the Governor's mansion, where the Prince awaited the evening's reception and entertainment.

It was the second night after his arrival that the reception was held for the native kings of Africa and some twenty of us who could make no claim to royal blood. I was curiously unmoved by the pomp and ceremony of the occasion and by the proud bearing of the Prince. Great fires were kindled in the gardens and native entertainers were brought to amuse the Prince. And although these Kaffirs did their utmost to play and dance and sing in a manner which would capture the fancy, there was little of the feeling of the native here and little of his wild rhythm. These natives were like children, frightened to think of the great personage before whom they were being exhibited. At last the Prince grew tired of the performance. At a wave of his hand the music died away and the dancing ceased.

Seeing the natives awe-struck and spellbound by the opulence of their conquerors, I felt defeat as never before. I realized that the English had secured a hold never to be broken, and that a man might waste his life in a futile attempt to change the situation without gaining so much as the sympathy of his own people. I began to feel that even Christianity with its lessons of forbearance and submission was hand in glove with imperialism. The unholy alliance between these two precluded the possibility of my accepting either.

Yet at this moment when all my efforts appeared fruitless and my life's quest hopelessly idealistic I was tantalized with a glimpse of the promised land. I saw a bare possibility of turning defeat to victory. Here were the kings of Africa gathered at Cape Town. Why not utilize the opportunity and bring them together in one great meeting? If harmony and good feeling could be engendered among them, old feuds would end, and the position of the native in South Africa would be immeasurably strengthened. If all the native tribes in South Africa could act as one unit, even the English would be forced to parley. The time was not yet ripe to form a Kaffir Union, but I saw the first step toward that possibility at hand.

The next morning I hurried to Bishop Coppin and outlined my proposed reception. He was enthusiastic over the idea, and called in F. Z. S. Peregrino and Reverend Mr. Gow to help us plan the affair. We worked energetically for three days and at last were ready.

When the night arrived, every important South African king with the exception of Segow Faku and Lerothodi was present. All my efforts in behalf of the former had failed to secure him an invitation to come to Cape Town. Lerothodi faced another obstacle. He was by far the most powerful native king in South Africa. For years his tribe had beaten both the Boers and the English, and even when the Basutos surrendered they had demanded the right to retain certain liberties and concessions unknown to their weaker neighbors. Because of his strength, the colonial officials were particularly anxious to keep Lerothodi from the meeting of the kings for fear that his influence might effect a coalition and work infinite harm to the colonial cause. He would have been the logical king of such a union. The English invited him to a small private reception at the Governor's mansion to be held on the same evening as our meeting. They knew that Lerothodi would not dare to refuse. They were right, but Lerothodi saw through their trick and although he could not come he sent his brother to represent Basutoland. We were forced to be satisfied.

Never, perhaps, was such a picturesque throng gathered under one roof. Here were eighteen full-blooded kings, who had fought among themselves all during their generation, perpetuating feuds which ran back to the very dawn of time. These men and their fathers had led their tribesmen through sub-tropical forests, down rivers, across karoo and veld to the sound of drums, and under the anger of old grievances fought terrible battles. Yet here they were, dressed as carefully as English gentlemen, with high top hats and Prince Albert coats, a little stiff perhaps in each other's presence, smouldering perhaps at the fierce eyes of a rival, but to all outward appearances polite and decorous. They were meeting for the first time to shake hands and become acquainted. The event was momentous. Here, if only the right words might be spoken and the right influences brought to bear, Ethiopia might be reinstated in all her former glory, or even better, lifted to a level of civilization more cultured, prosperous, and powerful than ever before.

Although the eighteen kings were dressed formally, their retainers and heirs apparent were arrayed in all their barbaric splendor. I was aware how thin the veneer of European culture actually was, and how thoroughly these people retained the characteristics of their race, characteristics quite as worthy as those the Europeans would force upon them.

Bishop Coppin made the address of welcome, and his deep voice filled the room. He finished by saying,

'African brethren, meet and converse and part as friends. The great God who watches all his children has not forgotten Ethiopia and he will lift you from misery if you will but love one another.'

The kings and their interpreters made replies to this speech. The strained silence of the early evening was broken, and the room gradually filled with the hum and mild thunder of many voices. A dozen dialects were spoken, some musical, some filled with the clicks which mark Hottentot derivation, some blended with Dutch and English. Kings became friendly, even jovial. We all banqueted on roast chicken, and scores of nicely browned birds disappeared as if by magic.

When we had finished eating, Bishop Coppin asked all of the kings, Peregrino, Reverend Mr. Gow, and me to step to the middle of the room. Here he had us join hands about him while he led us in his own song 'Ethiopia Stretch out Thy Hands' which had recently been set to music. The natives have a wonderful ear for music, and although most of them did not understand the words they all understood the melody and rhythm. By the third time through the eighteen kings and their three hundred retainers had joined in singing that Christian hymn. Again and again they sang it. The harmony grew wilder and more wild, the rhythm more and more barbaric. They drummed upon the table, they sang weird minor strains. Alto, bass, and tenor came deep and clear. And kings who had fought for untold generations held hands and sang a song which conquered even the most stubborn heart among them.

CHAPTER XXVIII

AH, SOUTH AFRICA, LAND OF VILLAINY, BLOOD, AND TEARS!

SOON after my return to Cape Town, matters began to shape themselves in such a way that I felt able to buy the rest of the materials for my concession in Basutoland. Price made himself very useful to me, and worked his way so thoroughly into my confidence that I trusted him more than I should have trusted any one. He was continually bringing me bargains of one sort or another, and he seemed so sincere in his efforts to help me that I gave him the power to make all the contracts for materials to be sent up to the Caledon River. I fully outlined the limits of my resources, never dreaming that he would willfully plunge me into debts I could not hope to erase. But ah, South Africa, land of villainy, blood, and tears, it was his sole aim to overwhelm me; it was his particular commission as a colonial official to ruin me and force me from South Africa.

It was many days, however, before I began to suspect him. The offer of backing which he and his bankers had made was renewed upon my return to Cape Town, and this more than anything else allayed my suspicion. I felt so secure and prosperous at this time that I had the Pedro Gorino put in dry dock for the installation of power. She had been making a good profit, but I realized that no sailing vessel could hope to compete with the power-driven ships which were becoming so numerous along the coast.

As payments came due on materials, however, my ready cash dwindled. This was no cause for alarm. I had a fortune in ostrich feathers locked in my warehouse. In my pocket were sixteen unregistered diamonds worth a small fortune. There was my ship the Pedro Gorino, and above all there was my concession in Basutoland merely awaiting a few shiploads of materials to develop its resources and make me independently wealthy. The lack of ready cash merely meant that I would have to sell the ostrich feathers or the diamonds, or negotiate a loan.

It was then that I told Price of my ostrich feathers, which was, I have no doubt, the opening he sought. My warehouse was a small one-story building of stone, several hundred feet behind my office. It was here that I was keeping my feathers awaiting the right market and the right price. When I found that I would have to sell, I wanted another's valuation on the plumes. It was for this reason that I took Price to see them. I opened one of the cases and took several A number one primes, the kind that buyers dream about. Price could not hide his amazement and when I asked him the value of my hoard he estimated it, as I had, at five thousand pounds.

It was late afternoon as we locked the warehouse behind us, and I was fully determined to sell the feathers on the following morning. I went to my office and began to figure rapidly. With the extra five thousand pounds, yes, I could make it. I would be able to pay for everything. My materials were ready to load aboard the Pedro Gorino. In five more days the ship would have power; no longer would it be at the mercy of the winds. I sat in my chair thinking and dreaming of the months to come. It would be hard to divide my time between the Pedro Gorino with its newly installed power and my concession employing seventy-five men. Within the year I could buy Lorenço Marques and the Portuguese Colony if the offer still held. I would show the imperialists that an Ethiopian could gain by fair means all that they were gaining by foul. Perhaps I fell asleep, for I remember dreaming of Africa as it had been before the ships from Europe reached her shores, an Arcadia with whole races living the quiet pastoral life of herdsmen, a country unravaged by war and inhabited by a people without lust for wealth or land. I saw forgotten nations laying their masonry at Khami and Zimbabwe, men of astonishing culture for that remote epoch.

I do not know how long I slept, but when I opened my eyes I found the room suffocating with the fumes of burning animal matter. Heavy black smoke was pouring in through an open window. My senses were still benumbed by sleep yet I thought intuitively of the feathers. I rushed out to my warehouse and stood speechless at the destruction going on before my eyes. The wooden roof of the little stone building was a mass of flame. The padlock was broken and through the open door I could see my priceless ostrich feathers poured from their cases into one great pile upon the floor and burning like so many autumn leaves. They must have been soaked in oil to have burned the way they did. There was nothing I could do. The goods were already ruined. A little group who had gathered as the flames were seen afar stood in the half-darkness with the light of the fire upon their faces. They laughed grotesquely, their vacant faces registered faint amusement. I stood apart, sharing my grief and my suspicions with no one. Because it was a tiny building at a safe distance from any other no one had been called to fight the fire. After the roof had collapsed the crowd began to move away; they were not interested now that the fire had died down.

I spent a sleepless night and returned to my office the next morning prepared to do what I could. Unfortunately my feathers had not been insured, and the burned goods were a total loss. My assets now consisted of a ship being held in dry dock awaiting payment for the installation of power, a concession in Basutoland which was mine to develop and to exploit, but not personal property in the eyes of the colonial officials and therefore not security for a loan, a sum in the bank insufficient to meet one tenth of my debts, sixteen diamonds which were unregistered and therefore impossible to sell except at a great risk, and a promise of a loan from men whom I was beginning to distrust. There were two possibilities. I could attempt to sell the diamonds or I could attempt to get the loan.

I determined upon a bold and dangerous stroke. Slipping the leather wallet which contained my sixteen rough diamonds into my pocket I walked down to the dock and looked out across the bay. A British mail steamer lay at anchor some distance out, and as it was early morning only a few passengers were as yet on deck. For some minutes I hesitated, telling myself that I was attempting a foolhardy feat, then renewing my resolve I hailed a boat and went aboard. For twenty minutes I wandered up and down the deck attempting to read the character of each I saw. There really was little choice. There was a lady of fifty, a boy of twelve, a group of young men and women, and an old fellow sitting in a deck chair reading his paper. More because the others were hopeless than for any other reason I picked the last mentioned.

The man whom I approached was an Englishman in his late fifties. He was slightly bald and stout with an expression akin to ferocity. Yet something within his eyes told me that beneath his forbidding exterior there was a gleam of humor and of sporting blood, a spark of sentiment and amiability. He would not have been my choice from among fifty but he seemed the most likely prospect, and I was not without hope.

I sat down beside him and began the conversation casually enough, 'How do you like South Africa?'

'This bloody weather,' he said.

'It's always chilly at this time of the year,' I explained. 'Now if you had come in January let us say. . . .'

'I ought to know,' he interrupted. 'I've been coming out here for twenty years.'

I was taken aback at his brusque manner and about to think better of mentioning the diamonds, but it was too late.

'What is it you want?' he asked.

I decided that there was nothing for it but to beard the lion in his den. 'I have in my pocket,' I said, 'sixteen rough diamonds which you can have for a quarter of their worth. If you don't care to buy them, I'll not take your time.'

As I had half expected, the shock cracked his rough shell. He was truly amazed and in a very different tone asked, 'I say, do you dare take this chance with the law what it is?'

For reply I pulled out the leather pouch, opened it, and having first made sure there were no other spectators, poured the diamonds into the cup of my hand for his examination.

He produced a monocle and surveyed them critically. 'A damn fine bunch of stones,' he said. 'I happen to know something about diamonds myself. Yes, I'll take them.' He began to feel for his billfold. 'I'll have to go to my stateroom for money,' he said.

A thousand surmises raced through my brain as I stood leaning with my back to the rail of the ship awaiting his return. I thought how easy it would be for him to betray me, and I remembered with apprehension that he had said that he knew something about diamonds himself. Several minutes slipped by. I was aware of my heart beating regularly, monotonously in my breast. How long he took!

At last he returned. My worst fears were realized. He was accompanied by two of the ship's officials, to whom he was talking with excitement. 'There he is now,' he said, pointing at me. 'I'll see that he gets the limit; this business has to be stopped.' They were still forty feet from me. It was a moment for quick thinking. The pouch containing the diamonds was in the pocket of my coat farthest from the Englishmen and therefore hidden from them. With as deft a movement as possible I lifted it from the pocket and with a flip dropped it into the bay behind me. Those sixteen stones are no doubt there to-day, a trifling addition to the enormous treasure scattered over the sea floor. I had not been detected. I was seized and searched, but there was not a stone on my person. They could do nothing but put me ashore.

These two catastrophes following closely one on the other, with payments due and no cash to meet them, made me resort to Price and his bankers. I had not seen Price since he had accompanied me to the warehouse to look at the feathers. More than ever I distrusted him. If he was a scoundrel, however, I wanted to assure myself of his nature. He and his bankers had promised to back me to the extent of twenty thousand pounds. I needed no such amount of money, but I did need five thousand badly. I still had my ship and my word as a gentleman.

I went to the cashier of the bank, told him my story, and asked if the offer they had made still held. He said that he felt sure a loan could be made and asked me to bring my papers the next afternoon. The next day at the appointed time I arrived at the bank. A liveried doorman took my hat and papers and I was shown into a room heavily draped and decorated. At a long, polished, mahogany table sat ten Englishmen, Price among them. I was not offered a chair, and for a moment there was a strained silence.

Then the president, roaring like a lion, burst forth, 'Captain Dean, do you think you can run South Africa?'

I was dumbfounded. I said, 'Price, what is the meaning of this?'

Price sat in cold silence while the president continued. 'You know very well the meaning,' he shouted. 'You're a diamond smuggler, an enemy of the British Government, and a damned American nigger. And if you aren't out of Cape Town within a week we'll put you on the Breakwater for evading your debts.'

I was so enraged I could scarcely control myself, but with an effort to be cool I asked, 'Are you the high tribunal? Has your illustrious government come to such a pass that it must place its judicature in the hands of bank clerks?'

'I am not here to be insulted,' the president thundered. 'You have maligned Cecil Rhodes, you have attempted to stir the Basutos, the Pondos and the Pondo Mesis to rise and massacre their English neighbors; in fact there is nothing you have not stooped to, and I demand an explanation.'

'It would be useless to explain,' I said wearily. 'You haven't the imagination to follow me, nor the philosophy to understand. I can assure you that all your accusations are false; I will not attempt more.'

'Then you refuse to account for your actions?'

'I have no reason to account to you for anything I have done.'

'Show him out, John. And remember, Dean, you have one week to get out of South Africa.'

I was shoved roughly to the street without my hat or my papers, nor was I ever able to recover them. Five days before, had I been treated in such a manner, I would have gone after my revolvers, but the succession of defeats had somewhat subdued my spirit. My bright dreams crashed about my head, and I knew that I must leave South Africa with my work unfinished. Under the Roman Dutch Law a man may be imprisoned for debt, and I realized that the bankers would be only too glad to see me on the Breakwater.

Then in my darkest days I was again befriended by Freighter and Elliott, who took the power of attorney over all my interests in South Africa, bought me a ticket for England on the British Mail steamer, and as an appreciation for old services gave me seventy-five pounds sterling on which to live.

The next morning I went down to the dock, called my crew together and told them the situation. I shook hands with all my men and dismissed them sadly. Sydney Wilson, Will Braithwaith, and I went over to see the Pedro Gorino where she lay in dry dock. She was newly painted a deep green with 'Pedro Gorino' lettered in white on her bow. Her masts stood proudly remembering old storms. And although no one spoke of it, we all were thinking that perhaps it was best to leave her thus, and never hear the angry rumble of an engine in her vitals, or see the wild, free spirit of her, broken and surly, and the ship plunging on without regard to wind or waves. And that was the last I ever saw of the Pedro Gorino.

Next morning I boarded the British Mail steamer and headed northward through the South Atlantic, driven from my motherland by foreigners and usurpers. I had no desire to go on to England, so I slipped ashore at Funchal, Madeira, a fugitive from justice. And I thought how like I was to Said Kafu and McKinnon Paige, who had come to Funchal a century and a half before. And like those two, I haunted the resorts of seamen that lie along that dirty, lively, wild, crescent bay, seeking passage aboard any ship for any country whatsoever.

THE END